◆ POCKET GUIDE ◆
TO THE
M·A·I·N·E
OUTDOORS

◆ POCKET GUIDE ◆
TO THE
M·A·I·N·E
OUTDOORS

EBEN THOMAS

THORNDIKE PRESS • THORNDIKE, MAINE

Library of Congress Cataloging in Publication Data

Thomas, Eben.
  Pocket guide to the Maine outdoors.

  1. Outdoor recreation—Maine.   2. Outdoor
recreation—Maine—Directories.   3. Maine—
Description and travel—1981-   —Guide-books.
I. Title.
GV191.42.M2T46   1985   917.41   85-9808
ISBN 0-89621-093-6 (soft)

Acknowledgments

Special appreciation to Paul Frinsko, Tom Shoener, Denny McNeish, the Dept. of Inland Fisheries and Wildlife, the Dept. of Marine Resources, and the Dept. of Conservation.

TABLE OF CONTENTS

WATER

LAND

GENERAL INFORMATION

WATER

(cont'd)

■ Canoeing

1 River Trips

There was a gusty old hunter from Milo, Maine, who once was accused of lying about the number of deer he had seen. "Not so," he replied. "I was enlarging upon the number to take into account those that were hiding in the grass and could not be seen."

The following maps and river descriptions have been excerpted from my three canoe books—*No Horns Blowing, Hot Blood and Wet Paddles,* and *The Weekender.* Rest assured unlike our friend from Milo if I have not seen it or paddled it, I will not write about it. To put it another way, as Fanny Hardy Eckstrom once said, "It is lovely to be beautiful but essential to be true."

So read on—then paddle!

For each trip you will find an accurate, up-to-date description including Forest Rangers to contact for fire permits, location and length of carries, location and difficulty of each set of rapids, and when necessary, which bank to make the carry.

I once wrote that paddling a white water river is like batting a bee out of the car window—panic takes hold until you get the hang of it. Just so you *can* get the knack, the rivers shown are listed in an *increasing* level of difficulty.

1. Saco River (N.H. to Rt. 5)
2. Saco River (Rt. 5 to East Brownfield)
3. Moose River (Bow River Trip)
4. West Branch Penobscot (Roll to Rip)
5. Blue Hill Falls
6. Nezinscot River
7. Wilson Stream
8. Sandy River
9. Cobbossee Stream
10. Sheepscot River
11. Aroostook River
12. Dead River (No. Branch)
13. Denny's River
14. Narraguagus River
15. St. Croix River
16. Allagash River
17 West Branch Penobscot to Ambajejus
18. Each Branch Penobscot
19. Machias River
20. St. John River

NOTE

1. Some of these listings could be interchanged, moved up or down one level perhaps, but I've tried to consider water levels and remoteness when making this list.
2. Heavy rains or late spring runoff could easily change the level of difficulty. Use common sense. Call the local forest ranger to ascertain water levels.

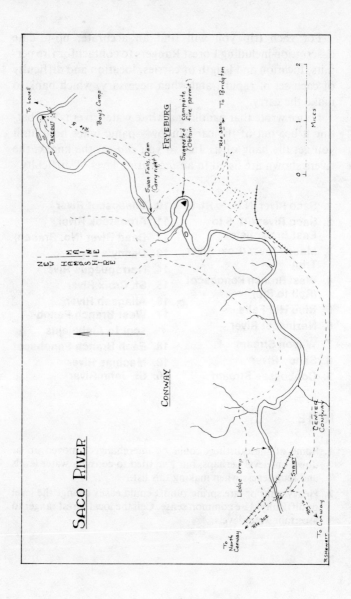

SACO RIVER

CONWAY

FRYEBURG

To Lowell

Takeout

Boy's Camp

Swan Falls Dam
(Carry right)

Suggested campsite
(Obtain fire permit)

Rte 302   To Bridgton

MAINE
NEW HAMPSHIRE

CENTER
CONWAY

Ledge Drop

START

Rte 16
To Conway

Rte 302

To
North
Conway

R.Stewart

0   1   2
MILES

1. SACO RIVER
N.H. to Rt. 5 Bridge

The Saco is everybody's river, a meld of smooth current, pure sand, and family fun.

Starting Point Arrive in Fryeburg, continue west past Maine/N.H. border, enter and leave Center Conway, bear right at fork of Rt. 16-302. Locate the abutments of an old covered bridge (burned in 1975). Launch on north side, upstream of bridge.

Campsites There are no authorized sites on this part of the river. Fire permits are needed and may be obtained from Forest Ranger, Fryeburg, ME 04037.

Car Shuttle From Fryeburg go 4 miles east on Rt. 5 to the Rt. 5 bridge, called "Canal Bridge." Leave a car in the picnic area.

Rapids & Carries 1/4 mile below the old bridge look for a gradual ledge drop. In high water only the white will show. In low times you may have to wade the canoes through—not a real tough spot, just be alert. Line or carry on right bank if you feel necessary.

The remainder of the paddle is through bright sand bars and a sandy, smooth-bottomed river of gentle current—great family place!

Plan to camp overnight at first good sand bar below Maine/N.H. border. See suggested site on map. Take out at Rt. 5 bridge.

Best Time to Canoe Late June, July, August.

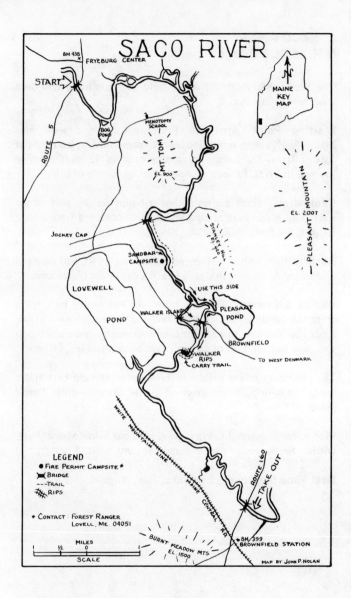

SACO RIVER

BM 438
x
FRYEBURG CENTER

START

MAINE KEY MAP

ROUTE 5

BOG POND

MENOTOMY SCHOOL

MT. TOM EL 900

PLEASANT MOUNTAIN

EL. 2007

JOCKEY CAP

STANLEY HILL EL. 460

SANDBAR CAMPSITE

USE THIS SIDE

LOVEWELL POND

WALKER ISLAND

PLEASANT POND

BROWNFIELD

TO WEST DENMARK

WALKER RIPS

CARRY TRAIL

WHITE MOUNTAIN LINE

MAINE CENTRAL RR

ROUTE 160

TAKE OUT

LEGEND
● Fire Permit Campsite *
⋈ Bridge
--- Trail
✕✕✕ Rips

✱ Contact: Forest Ranger
Lovell, Me. 04051

MILES
½   0
SCALE

BURNT MEADOW MTS. EL. 1500

✱ BM 399
BROWNFIELD STATION

MAP BY: JOHN P. NOLAN

2. SACO RIVER
Rt. 5 Bridge to East Brownfield

Starting Point   Upstream of Rt. 5 bridge on the west shore.

Campsites   There is only one authorized site, located at Walker Rips. All others require fire permits. Obtain from Forest Ranger, Fryeburg, ME 04037.

Car Shuttles   Drive from Fryeburg southeast on Rt. 5/113 about 8 miles to East Brownfield. Park on east side of river. An alternate take out point could be Lovewell Pond at the public boat launch in the southwest corner. You should reach the lake from the river by paddling up the outlet stream several miles below Walker Rips. Keep sharp eye out on the right bank for this stream. It is hard to see since it enters at an angle.

Rapids & Carries   With the possible exception of Walker Rips (see map) there are no rapids or carries. The rips are a short, often shallow set of easy Class I-II rapids some 100' in length. They may be easily carried on left bank.

A good campsite can be obtained by stopping at a convenient sand bar below Rt. 302 (road to Jockey Cap). Paddling below Walker Rips is easy all the way to East Brownfield. Take out below bridge on left bank.

Best Time to Canoe   Late June, July, August.

3. MOOSE RIVER
Bow River Trip

Starting Point   Approaching Jackman from the south, turn left off Rt. 201 just south of Rt. 201 and 6/15 Junction. This gravel road will lead to a public landing on the thoroughfare between Attean and Big Wood Pond. No shuttles are necessary if you start here, for the essence of the "Bow" is a complete circle back to the starting point.

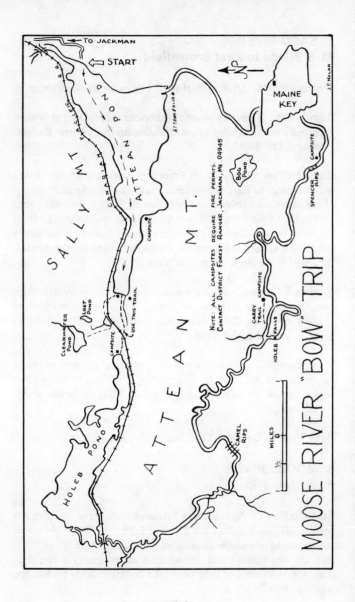

MOOSE RIVER "BOW" TRIP

TO JACKMAN
START
MAINE
J.P. NOLAN
SALLY MT.
CANADIAN PACIFIC
ATTEAN POND
ATTEAN FALLS
BOG POND
CAMPSITE
SPENCER RIPS
CAMPSITE
CLEARWATER POND
LOST POND
USE THIS TRAIL
CAMPSITE
ATTEAN MT.
CARRY TRAIL
CAMPSITE
HOLEB FALLS
HOLEB POND
CAMEL RIPS

Note: All campsites require fire permits.
Contact District Forest Ranger, Jackman, Me. 04945

MILES
0   1/2

Campsites   Fire permit required, request permits from: District Forest Ranger, Jackman, ME 04945.

Car Shuttle   None. This is the Bow River trip where you return to your starting point.

Rapids & Carries   This is not a difficult whitewater trip. With the exception of Attean Falls, all of the canoeable rapids are easy Class I—weak Class II. It is a wild remote area with some pretty scenery.

Carries   1. On west end of Attean Pond, carry trail to Holeb Pond leaves from rear of a sand beach on extreme west end of small cove. An old lumber road (1 ¼ miles) goes over railroad tracks to Holeb.

2. The major obstacle is Holeb Falls. Water cascades twenty-five feet in wild abandon so really think about locating the carry spot, which can be a bit obscured. There has been a camp stuck on a ledge on the right bank. This should serve as a marker. The Falls are about one mile below. As you approach the island in front of the Falls, bear left but keep close to the island. Do not enter the stream just north of the island. This is a dead end. Pass through short rock section, then one with rocks close on both sides. *Pass* the next lagoon on left, *enter* the next which leads to carry trail. If in doubt here, go to shore and scout around—don't mess around. It is twenty-five feet straight down! (**Note:** In 1984 there were a large number of blow-downs on the left shore. These could obscure the trail.)

Mosquito Rips lie ¼ mile below Holeb. Class II—can be sharp in shallow water. Four miles below Mosquito you will encounter Spencer Rips, which is a Class II short set of rips. You can portage left if in doubt.

Seven miles of dead water lie below Spencer to Attean Falls. Attean is a double drop with pool in between, a Class II–III section. If you need to carry, do the upper on the left and lower on right.

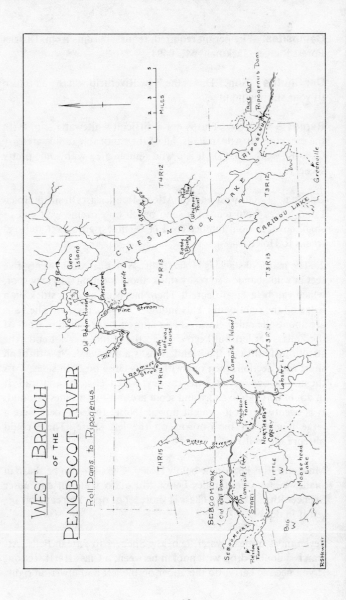

WEST BRANCH
OF THE
PENOBSCOT RIVER
Roll Dams to Ripogenus

0 1 2 3 4 5
MILES

T3R13
Gero Island
Chesuncook
Old Boom House
Pine Stream
Campsite
Sandy Bay
T4R13
Red Brook
Mud Pond
Weymouth Point
Ripogenus Dam
Take Out
T4R12
Chesuncook Lake
Ripogenus
T3R12
Greenville
Caribou Lake
T3R13
Little Brook
Smith Halfway House
Redmutt Stream
T4R14
Campsite (Island)
Lobster L.
T3R14
Russell Stream
Penobscot Farm
Nesowadnehunk
Campsite (Cove)
Seboomook
Old Roll Dams
T4R15
Little W
Moosehead Lake
Big W
Seboomook
Pittston Farm
Start

R.S. Hewitt

Generally these can be run, and make a fitting end after that seven miles of dead water. Continue across Attean Lake to your car.

Best Time to Canoe   Late May, June, July.

4. WEST BRANCH PENOBSCOT
Roll Dam to Rip Dam

Starting Point   Drive to Greenville, then NW to Rockwood, then north across bridge over Moose River through the stone pillars of Great Northern. Drive 40 miles over good gravel to Seboomook, then follow signs to Roll Dam two miles downstream from lake outlet.

Campsites   Sites along this corridor are subject to change. Some are fire permit, others are authorized. Best plan here is to check with Forest Ranger, Moosehead District H.Q., Greenville, ME 04441.

Car Shuttles   You will need separate, nontrip shuttle drivers who should go all the way to Roll Dam and unload you. They would then return to Seboomook Dam, cross the dam to the Golden Road intersection, turn right, follow Golden Road approximately 28 miles to foot of Caribou Lake. Here they would bear left to Ripogenus Dam and leave car there.

Rapids & Carries   There are some mixed easy current and mild Class I rapids just below Roll Dam which quickly riffle out to slow current or still water. This continues from Russell Stream to Big Island (just below Smith's halfway house). Easy Class I–II rapids may be easily run on the right side of the Island and end just below. Flowage from the lake will be quickly encountered making it all flat to the lake. (If *extreme* low water should prevail signs of a ledge drop may be seen at Pine Stream but this is unlikely.) The remaining paddle is over Chesuncook to Ripogenus Dam.

Best Time to Canoe   Late May, June, July, August, Sept.

11

Eben Thomas photo.

5. BLUE HILL FALLS

This is a trip only because you drive here, but a wild, fantastic day is in store for you. Blue Hill is the site of reversing tidal water action that creates Class IV standing waves without rocks. Pick a sunny day and get to the Stevens Bridge 2 hours before high tide. The best runs are made 2 hours before and 2 hours after high tide.

Starting Point   Going east on Rt. 1 from Bucksport, turn right in East Orland on Rt. 15. Follow 15 to Blue Hill. Turn right on 15 in Blue Hill to Junction 172/175, turn right on 172/175. Take 175 where road forks to the cement bridge with "Stevens" carved at the top. Spread your beach towels below the bridge on the Blue Hill side.

Campsites   None.

Car Shuttles   None.

Rapids & Carries   No carries. When the tide is coming *in* launch on the bay side of the bridge, paddle out to the high stacking waves in the center above the bridge. Try canoe, kayaks, or innertubes, for the wildest ride of your life. Near the end of the stacks work your way to the right to break the current line, then let the eddy work you back to the bridge. Then do it all over again! At high tide the water becomes absolutely flat—that's the time to eat. Outgoing tide brings great fun below the bridge after about two hours. It is interesting to see the water build in volume as the tide retreats. **Note:**   This is moving salt water and can be cold. Keep a canoe available to retrieve people who don't break the current line and are a long way from shore. If you have a wet suit top, bring it.

Best Time to Canoe   Any warm, sunny day 2 hours before high tide.

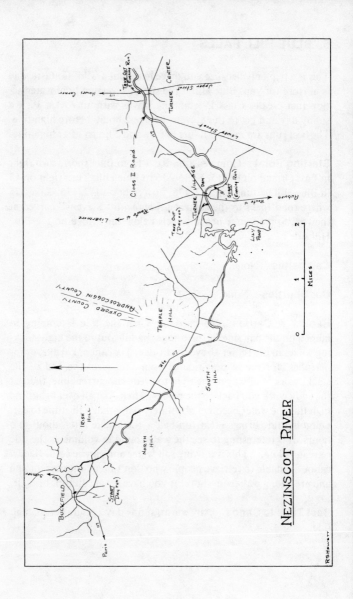

NEZINSCOT RIVER

R.S. Hewett

6. NEZINSCOT RIVER

The Nezinscot is a lazy, pastoral river with some surprisingly alert sections to keep you honest. This is still a family river with easy Class I–II rapids.

Starting Point   Arrive via Rt. 4 or Rt. 117 to town of Turner. Locate the dam in town and launch on the right bank downstream alongside the large store.

Campsites   There are no authorized sites or fire permits available. This is a short morning or afternoon paddle and campsites are really not needed.

Car Shuttle   Leave one car at the second (easterly) Rt. 117 bridge (see map). Park on the upstream left bank.

Rapids & Carries   The launch site puts you right into easy, shallow, Class I rapids for 200 yards. These riffle out to open deadwater which continues for the next several miles. Then the river tilts and freshens up to Class II. There are no traps or sharp drops, and the shallowness allows you to recover from any "poor judgment."

Scout the small ledge drop and rapids immediately below the Route 117 bridge in Turner Center. Run the main vee of water over the ledge. In low water the next 100 yards is a shallow, head sized boulder patch which you may need to wade. In high water this is a short but fun canoeing spot. Small intermittent riffles continue to the next bridge. Take out upstream on left bank.

Best Time to Canoe   Mid-April, to third week in May or after heavy rain.

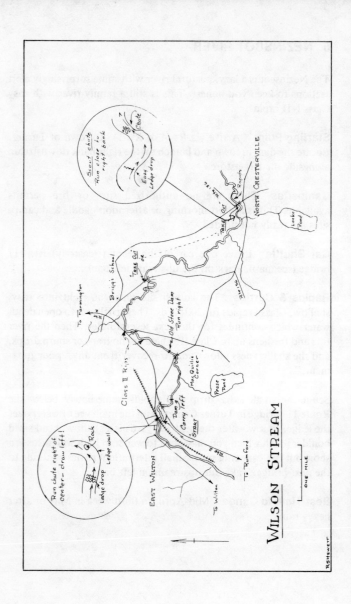

WILSON STREAM

ONE MILE

NORTH CHESTERVILLE

Locker Pond

Take Out

Rte 43

Briggs School

To Farmington

Old Stone Dam
Run right

MacQuillis Corner

Pease Pond

Class II Rips

Rte 2

East Wilton

Dam
Carry left

START

Rte 2

To Rumford

To Wilton

Scout chute
Run close to
right bank

Chute

Easy
Ledge drop

Run chute right of
center-draw left!

Rock

Ledge drop

Ledge wall

R.S.HEWETT

16

7. WILSON STREAM

Wilson is the ideal beginners river. If offers a ledge drop, rapids, and an old dam for the paddler to negotiate, but all at a reduced level. Experience can be gained and confidence built on Wilson.

Starting Point   Drive SW on Rt. 2 from Farmington or NE on Rt. 2 from Rumford, Rt. 4 from the south. Arrive at East Wilton. Locate the dam, then launch below the railroad tracks on the right bank.

Campsites   There are no fire permits available or authorized sites. Plan this as a day trip.

Car Shuttles   There are two options: If you run the whole trip, leave a car at the bridge in North Chesterville. A shortened trip can be arranged by taking the small road off Rt. 2 known as Knowlton Corner Road (road to Briggs School). Take the first right on this road (gravel) and go a short way to bridge. (See canoe map.)

Rapids & Carries   Depending on your adventuresome spirit there are no carries unless you choose to carry the cement dam about 1/2 mile below launch site. Within the first 1/4 mile, look for sharp dogleg by left with small ledge drop and rapids. Run this top part right of center, then center. (See insert canoe map.) If you kneel, everything works out nicely! Now watch for the dam mentioned above—either run or carry. The dam has a notch in the center where spillway doors have been. Run over the notch. If you choose to carry do so on the left bank. This is just a lift around spot.

Just below second bridge, scout from left bank the area marked on canoe map as Old Stone Dam. Run this on extreme right through small chute. Note areas above and below next bridge—shallow but sporty Class II rapids—great spot.

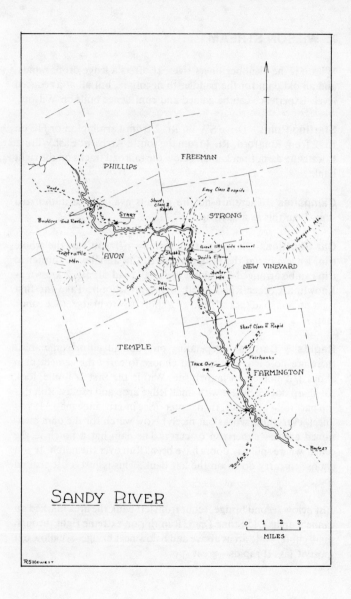

SANDY RIVER

PHILLIPS

FREEMAN

STRONG

Route 4

Easy Class II rapids

Short Class II Rapids

"Start"

Boulders and Rocks

AVON

Rattle Mtn

Spruce Mountain

Day Mtn

Slabb Mtn

Great little side channel

Devils Elbow

Hunter Mtn

NEW VINEYARD

New Vineyard Mtn

TEMPLE

Short Class II Rapid

Route 2

TAKE OUT OR

Fairbanks

FARMINGTON

Route 2

Route 27

0 1 2 3
MILES

R.S.Hewett

Take out at next bridge downstream on right bank or paddle six miles through flat water. Just above North Chesterville, there is a ledge drop and chute, Class II. Run ledge on right and chute far right (see map). Take out upstream of bridge.

Best Time to Canoe   Mid-April to third week in May or after heavy rain.

8. SANDY RIVER

The Sandy is a meandering river full of excitement, with rapids up to easy Class II.

Starting Point   Arrive in Phillips (north of Farmington on Rt. 4) and go east over the bridge. The Sandy here is a wild boulder strewn section which is uncanoeable. Turn right on Rt. 149, go 2.2 miles. Look for a small storage-type building on the left. Drive right into small road directly opposite this building—short drive to shore.

Campsites   Plan this as a day trip as land along the entire shore is privately owned and fire permits are unavailable. There are no authorized sites.

Car Shuttles   Leave a car at either the bridge in downtown Farmington or at Fairbanks bridge on Rt. 4.

Rapids & Carries   There are no carries. Rapids are open with no places that jam a canoe. Level of difficulty never exceeds Class II. See canoe map for location of rapids. While Devil's Elbow sounds menacing there is no problem in the river.

Note of Caution: Rapids are not a problem on this river but flooding can be. Check this out before canoeing. Sharp turns and overhanging trees can be dangerous in high, flooded conditions.

Best Time to Canoe   Mid-April to Mid-May.

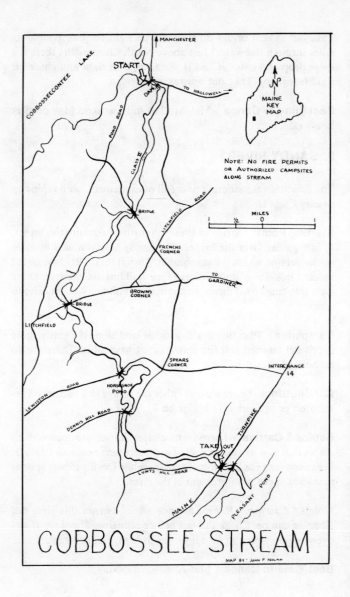

START

COBBOSSEECONTEE LAKE

MANCHESTER

DAM

TO HALLOWELL

MAINE KEY MAP

NP

NOTE: NO FIRE PERMITS OR AUTHORIZED CAMPSITES ALONG STREAM

POND ROAD

CLASS II

MILES
½   0

BRIDGE

LITCHFIELD ROAD

FRENCHS CORNER

TO GARDINER

BROWNS CORNER

BRIDGE

LITCHFIELD

SPEARS CORNER

INTERCHANGE 14

LEWISTON ROAD

HORSESHOE POND

DENNIS HILL ROAD

MAINE TURNPIKE

TAKE OUT

LUNTS HILL ROAD

PLEASANT POND

COBBOSSEE STREAM

MAP BY: JOHN P. NOLAN

20

9. COBBOSSEE STREAM

Images of Indian voyages flow along the river banks. This was once a major Indian route from interior Maine to saltwater summer hunting and fishing grounds.

Starting Point   From Augusta follow Rt. 202 west to Manchester, turn left onto the Pond Road. Drive approximately 4 miles to the outlet bridge. Park on the south side, launch on the lake side of the road.

Campsites   There are no campsites available since the river runs through private property.

Car Shuttles   From the launch point, drive 2¼ miles to first intersection, turn left for 2¼ miles, park on west side of bridge. The old dam, the take out point, is visible from the bridge.

Rapids & Carries   From the lake, enter a short flowage to the outlet dam. Lift around this on right bank. In high water the current will be fast here below the dam with water into the trees. One hundred yards of Class I rapids leads to a dogleg right and a flatwater section. This is followed by a narrow river with fast current and small riffles to a wide deadwater pond. Listen—sharp (bony when water is low) Class II rapids run continuously for a quarter mile. Scout this from the right bank and from the snowmobile bridge about 100 yards down from the top.

There are no suggested routes since water levels change the course. Expect everything from high standing waves to a bony rock garden. The rapids riffle out into a small pond. Take out right shore above the broken dam. *Do not* run the dam!

Best Time to Canoe   Mid-April to mid-May or after heavy rain.

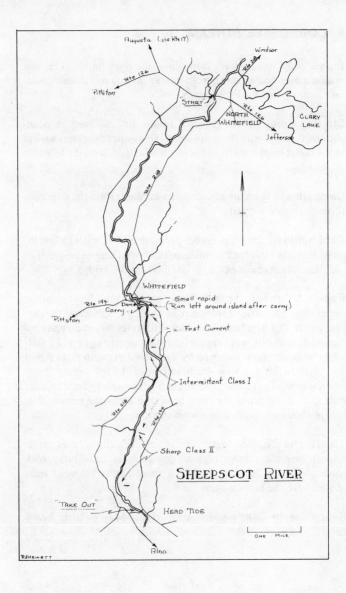

Augusta (via Rte 17)

Windsor

Rte 28

Rte 126

Pittston

"START"

Rte 126

NORTH
WHITEFIELD

CLARY
LAKE

Jefferson

Rte 28

WHITEFIELD

Rte 194

Dam

Small rapid
(Run left around island after carry)

Carry

Pittston

Fast Current

Intermittent Class I

Rte 28

Rte 194

Sharp Class II

SHEEPSCOT RIVER

"TAKE OUT"

HEAD TIDE

ONE MILE

Alna

R.SHEWETT

22

10. SHEEPSCOT RIVER

It is difficult to believe that a twelve mile canoe trip as pretty as this is available in central Maine.

Starting Point   Follow I-95 to Augusta, go south on west side of Kennebec to Gardiner, cross the river to Randolph, follow 126 to North Whitefield. Launch on the west shore upstream of bridge.

Campsites   No fire permit or authorized sites—day trip only.

Car Shuttles   From the west side, drive south six miles on the Townhouse Road, then six more miles south on Rt. 218 to the dam in Headtide.

Rapids & Carries   North Whitefield to Whitefield—there are no carries in this section. There are no real rapids either, rather fast current and shallow riffles. Just below Rt. 194 bridge there is a small Class I rapid—go to right bank after this and carry 100 yards around a series of large ledge drops. Put in just below last ledge, paddle across the river left around the island. There are no hidden problems behind the island.

Flat water for next three miles, then two miles of continuous Class II. Very sporty—take out right bank at dam in Headtide.

Best Time to Canoe   Mid-April to third week in May or after heavy rain.

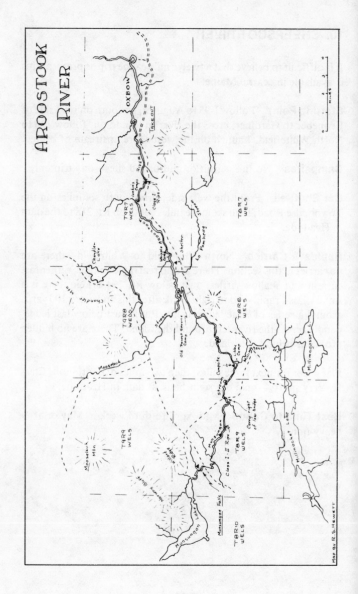

AROOSTOOK RIVER

Map by R. S. Hewett

11. AROOSTOOK RIVER

Fine rapids and wild country are good descriptions of the Aroostook.

Starting Point   It is possible to drive to junction of the Pinkham Road and Munsungan Stream but the roads are long (Telos Road, same access road used to enter Allagash, then Pinkham Road) and dusty. I recommend you make this a fly-in trip. (See Bush Pilots.)

Campsites   All sites require fire permits which should be requested from Maine Forest Service, Masardis, ME 04759.

Car Shuttles   Most air outfits will, for a small fee, shuttle your car to the take out point—*great service!*

Rapids and Carries   In the section between Little Munsungan and Munsungan Falls there are some small Class I & II rumpled rapids around Willard Brook. Just above Munsungan Falls there is a series of short ledge drops. The last two are about 100 yards apart, and the last one is 30 yards above the lip of the Falls. These may be shallow and "toothy"—plan to run left of center or line over them. Take out left above Munsungan Falls (approx. 8′ drop) and carry around this drop.

Below Munsungan watch for trees in the river in the meandering section, then intermittent Class I-II rapids. The five miles above and below the low bridge are full of gentle falling rapids—outstanding paddle section.

From Libby Camp to Oxbow, there are only a few spaced rapids of Class I vintage. Take out at Oxbow—right bank.

Best Time to Canoe   Mid-May to mid-June.

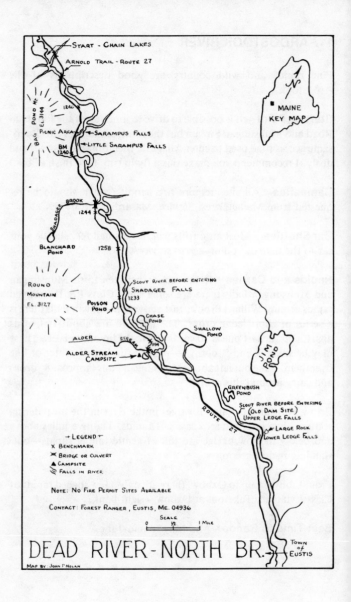

START - CHAIN LAKES

ARNOLD TRAIL - ROUTE 27

MAINE
KEY MAP

BAG POND MT.
EL. 3144

1246

PICNIC AREA
SARAMPUS FALLS
LITTLE SARAMPUS FALLS

BM
1240

SHADAGEE BROOK
1244

BLANCHARD POND

1258

ROUND MOUNTAIN
EL. 3127

SCOUT RIVER BEFORE ENTERING
SHADAGEE FALLS
1233

POISON POND

CHASE POND

SHALLOW POND

ALDER STREAM
1194

ALDER STREAM CAMPSITE

JIM POND

GREENBUSH POND

ROUTE 27

SCOUT RIVER BEFORE ENTERING
(OLD DAM SITE)
UPPER LEDGE FALLS

LARGE ROCK
LOWER LEDGE FALLS

LEGEND

X BENCHMARK
✕ BRIDGE OR CULVERT
▲ CAMPSITE
≋ FALLS IN RIVER

NOTE: No FIRE PERMIT SITES AVAILABLE

CONTACT: FOREST RANGER, EUSTIS, ME. 04936

SCALE
0   ½   1 MILE

DEAD RIVER - NORTH BR.

TOWN OF EUSTIS

MAP BY: JOHN P. NOLAN

12. DEAD RIVER (North Branch)

Very historic. This river was used by Benedict Arnold on his way to attack Quebec during the American Revolution.

Starting Point　Take Rt. 27 to Eustis. Ask in town where to locate the obscure gravel road to the dam at the foot of Chain of Ponds. Short gravel road goes directly to the lake.

Campsite　There are no authorized sites and no fire permits available on the river. Plan to set up a base camp at Natanis Point at north end of Chain of Ponds (a private fee site), or Cathedral Pines in Eustis (private fee site—hot showers).

Car Shuttles　Ask in town for the landing in Eustis off Rt. 27, and leave a car here. Then continue up Rt. 27 to starting point.

Rapids and Carries　Starting at the dam you cruise through shallow, easy Class I rapids, pass under Rt. 27. In one mile prepare to carry Sarampus Falls (approx. 8′ drop), short carry on right. Below pool, paddle Little Sarampus (small runnable ledge drop).

Four miles downstream watch for Shadagee Falls, a sharp Class II-III ledge drop. Scout from right bank—runnable in right water. Then three miles of flat water to an old wood dam called "Old Ledge Falls Dam." In normal water this is a Class II drop followed by several hundred yards of Class II rapids. Now watch for Ledge Falls, a sharp Class II to III drop. You can scout this drop from Rt. 27. Run just right of rock. Class II next 200 yards, then riffles and flat water to Eustis.

Best Time to Canoe　Mid-May to early July.

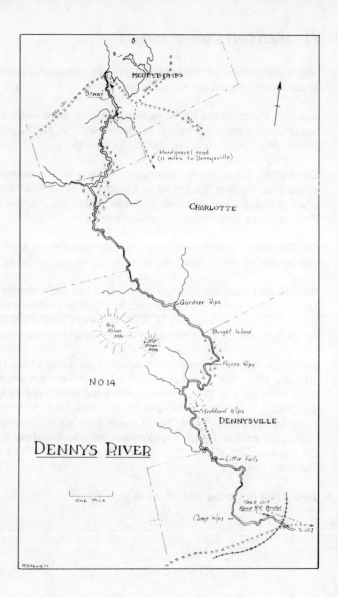

MEDDYBEMPS

Start

Rte 191

Rte 214

Rte 214

Hard gravel road
(11 miles to Dennysville)

CHARLOTTE

Gardner Rips

Big
Allan
Mtn

Little
Allan
Mtn

Bright Island

Ayers Rips

NO 14

Stoddard Rips

DENNYSVILLE

DENNYS RIVER

Little Falls

ONE MILE

"TAKE OUT
Above RR Bridge"

Camp Rips

To US1

R.SHEWETT

28

13. DENNYS RIVER

A sparkling river full of surprises and exciting paddling.

Starting Point Arrive in Bangor, cross over to Brewer, then Rt. 9 through Beddington to Wesley, Crawford and Alexander, then south eight miles to Meddybemps. Launch on east shore below the dam.

Campsites All sites require a fire permit. Request these from Maine Forest Service, Meddybemps, ME 04657.

Car Shuttles Drive to Dennysville via Rt. 214 to Charlotte, Ayers and Rt. 1, then south on Rt. 1 to Dennysville. Ask in town where the railroad bridge is located and park cars there. *Do not canoe below this bridge*—wild stuff there!

Rapids & Carries There are no carries with the possible exception of Little Falls. All rapids in early spring are Class II, some sharp Class II. Rapids such as Gardiner Rips, Ayers Rips (Class II) are mixed in with other Class II runs so it becomes difficult to pinpoint your location on this trip. Do keep an eye out below Stoddard Rips and the Whaleback for Little Falls. This is a Class III spot. In the right water levels, it can be run. If you plan this approach run right of center. This can be a tough run for loaded canoes, so plan ahead! Carries can be made on the left bank (100 yards). Clear sailing to your take out location.

Best Time to Canoe Late April to third week in May.

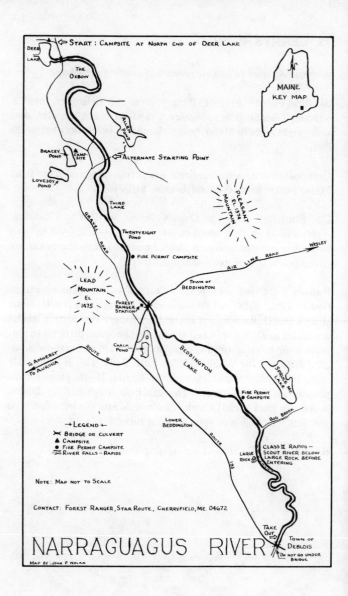

START: CAMPSITE AT NORTH END OF DEER LAKE

DEER LAKE

THE OXBOW

MAINE KEY MAP

ALLEN POND

BRACEY POND

CAMPSITE

ALTERNATE STARTING POINT

LOVEJOY POND

PLEASANT MOUNTAIN EL. 1374

THIRD LAKE

GRAVEL ROAD

TWENTYEIGHT POND

FIRE PERMIT CAMPSITE

AIR LINE ROAD

WESLEY

LEAD MOUNTAIN EL. 1475

TOWN OF BEDDINGTON

FOREST RANGER STATION

CHALK POND

BEDDINGTON LAKE

TO AMHERST TO AURORA

ROUTE 9

SPRUCE MT. LAKE

FIRE PERMIT CAMPSITE

LOWER BEDDINGTON

ROUTE 193

BOG BROOK

CLASS II RAPIDS – SCOUT RIVER BELOW LARGE ROCK BEFORE ENTERING

LARGE ROCK

—+ LEGEND +—

⋈ BRIDGE OR CULVERT
▲ CAMPSITE
● FIRE PERMIT CAMPSITE
≋ RIVER FALLS – RAPIDS

NOTE: MAP NOT TO SCALE

CONTACT: FOREST RANGER, STAR ROUTE, CHERRYFIELD, ME. 04672

TAKE OUT

TOWN OF DEBLOIS

Do not go under bridge

NARRAGUAGUS RIVER

MAP BY: JOHN P. NOLAN

14. NARRAGUAGUS RIVER

Starting Point   Take Rt. 9 east from the Bangor area, drive to Forest Ranger Station where Rt. 9 crosses the river. The Narraguagus can be canoed all the way from Deer Lake, but I suggest you avoid the section below Deer Lake. Beaver dams and dri-ki can make this section difficult. See alternate starting point on map or ask the Ranger for best location.

Campsites   There are two authorized sites, Deer Lake, and Bracey Pond. Fire permits are normally written for campsites at Twenty-Eight Mile Pond and at the foot of Beddington Lake (east side). Request from: Forest Ranger, Star Route, Cherryfield, ME 04672.

Car Shuttles   Turn right at the Forest Ranger Station (noted above) onto Rt. 193. Drive 8 miles to the bridge at Deblois. Leave a car on the west side of the bridge.

Carries & Rapids   The Narraguagus flows easily from the starting point. Mostly Class I rapids. There is an easy set that has a small Class II ledge drop about a mile above the Rt. 9 bridge. Small riffles extend into Beddington Lake. An old Atlantic salmon fish tagging station sits at the foot of the lake. Run the small one foot drop out of the holding pool, then current and Class I rapids for four miles. Be ready here for several sharp Class II runs. Watch for huge rock on right bank. This marks the only Class III location. Scout from right bank. Two miles of exciting Class II rapids follow to an easy Class II-III ledge drop. Small rapids and current remains to bridge at Deblois. Take out right above bridge. *Uncanoeable rapids* lie below bridge.

Best Time to Canoe   Late April to third week in May.

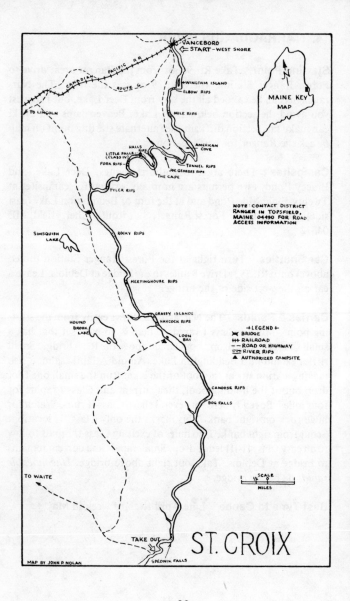

VANCEBORO
START - WEST SHORE

MAINE KEY MAP

CANADIAN PACIFIC R.R.

ROUTE 6

TO LINCOLN

WINGDAM ISLAND
ELBOW RIPS

MILE RIPS

AMERICAN COVE

HALLS RIPS
LITTLE FALLS (CLASS II)
FORK RIPS
THE CAPE
TUNNEL RIPS
JOE GEORGES RIPS

TYLER RIPS

NOTE: CONTACT DISTRICT RANGER IN TOPSFIELD, MAINE 04490 FOR ROAD ACCESS INFORMATION

SIMSQUISH LAKE

ROCKY RIPS

MEETINGHOUSE RIPS

GRASSY ISLANDS
HAYCOCK RIPS
LOON BAY

HOUND BROOK LAKE

+ LEGEND +
✕ BRIDGE
╫ RAILROAD
--- ROAD OR HIGHWAY
≈≈≈ RIVER RIPS
▲ AUTHORIZED CAMPSITE

CANOOSE RIPS

DOG FALLS

TO WAITE

TAKE OUT

SPEDNIK FALLS

ST. CROIX

SCALE
0 5
MILES

MAP BY JOHN P. NOLAN

32

15. ST. CROIX RIVER

My choice for *best all around family paddling*. Children 12 and over can act as paddlers with an experienced stern paddler.

Starting Point   Rt. 95 to Lincoln—Rt. 6 to Vanceboro. Put in behind Monk's General Store in town.

Campsites   You'll need only one if planning to take out at Loon Bay, and I suggest you take out here. Site is at Little Falls. You may camp at the Falls, or on the flat shore below Falls. Fire permit required—request from Forest Ranger, Topsfield, ME. 04490. Loon Bay is an authorized site.

Car Shuttles   The roads here can be confusing and bumpy. I would recommend you hire the shuttle from Monk's Store in Vanceboro. He has a very reasonable fee and having him do the driving will make your whole trip more pleasant. Write to Richard Monk, Vanceboro, ME 04491.

Rapids & Carries   You start in a set of easy, open, Class II rapids for 200 yards, then flat water to a series of easy Class II rapids: Elbow Rips, Mile Rips, Tunnel Rips, Joe Georges Rips, and Hall's Rips. These are generally full of waves but few rocks.

Land on the right bank at Little Falls. These are Class III to IV ledge drops, very exciting to run with an additional challenge to the left of a small island (to Class II-III). Outstanding campsite here.

The next day the river runs over shallow rapids which require some rock picking but never exceeds Class II. Watch for Tyler Rips, Rocky Rips (best, longest of trip), Meetinghouse Rips, Haycock Rips (sharp S turn). The St. Croix riffles out to flat water at Loon Bay. Take out on right shore.

Best Time to Canoe   Late May, June, July, August, Sept. (dam-controlled water).

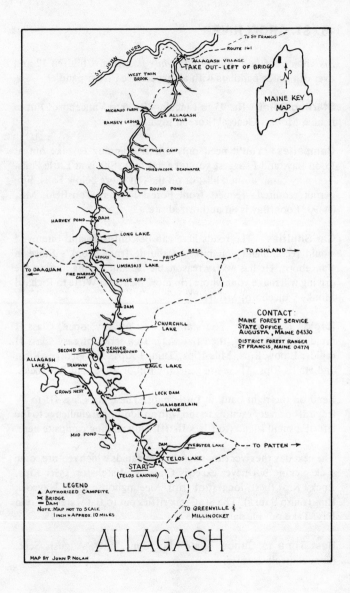

TO ST FRANCIS

ST JOHN RIVER

ROUTE 161

ALLAGASH VILLAGE
TAKE OUT ~ LEFT OF BRIDGE

WEST TWIN
BROOK

MAINE KEY
MAP

N↑

MICHAUD FARM
RAMSEY LEDGES

ALLAGASH FALLS

FIVE FINGER CAMP

MUSQUACOOK DEADWATER

ROUND POND

HARVEY POND ~ DAM

LONG LAKE

LEDGES

PRIVATE ROAD

TO ASHLAND →

UMSASKIS LAKE

TO DAAQUAM ←

FIRE WARDEN
CAMP

CHASE RIPS

DAM

CHURCHILL
LAKE

CONTACT:
MAINE FOREST SERVICE
STATE OFFICE
AUGUSTA, MAINE 04330

DISTRICT FOREST RANGER
ST FRANCIS, MAINE 04774

SECOND RIDGE

ZEIGLER
CAMPGROUND

ALLAGASH
LAKE

TRAMWAY

EAGLE LAKE

CROWS NEST

LOCK DAM

CHAMBERLAIN
LAKE

MUD POND

DAM

WEBSTER LAKE

TO PATTEN →

START
(TELOS LANDING)

TELOS LAKE

LEGEND
▲ AUTHORIZED CAMPSITE
✕ BRIDGE
▬ DAM
NOTE: MAP NOT TO SCALE
1 INCH = APPROX 10 MILES

TO GREENVILLE &
MILLINOCKET

ALLAGASH

MAP BY JOHN P. NOLAN

34

16. ALLAGASH RIVER

This is Maine's most recognized river. The map shown is presented to give you an idea of the mix of lakes and interconnecting river corridors. For accurate canoeing you should request the detailed map and guide available from:

> Allagash Wilderness Waterway
> Bureau of Parks & Recreation
> Dept. of Conservation
> State House Station #22
> Augusta, ME 04333

This guide will address most questions you will have including: outline of trip with distances between campsites, access to waterway, parking, gear, assistance, and telephone numbers for more help.

Some quick basic facts about the river:

1. Total trip from Telos to Allagash Village is approximately 100 miles.
2. Level of difficulty—up to Class II.
3. Most people plan seven to ten days to travel this water.
4. There are seventy-five fire safe authorized campsites clearly marked with a triangular sign.
5. Camping and fire building is authorized only at these sites.
6. Registration is required and can be done at various entry points or with any Park Ranger you might meet.
7. Group size is limited to twelve persons.

Topo Maps Needed   Allagash, Round Pond, Allagash Falls, Umsaskis Lake, Musquacook Lakes, Allagash Lake, Churchill Lake, Spider Lake, Chesuncook, and Telos Lake.

Car Shuttles   As the late Marshall Dodge related in one of his famous Bert & I routines, "You can't get there from here." Car shuttles on the Allagash are equally difficult. The best plan is to

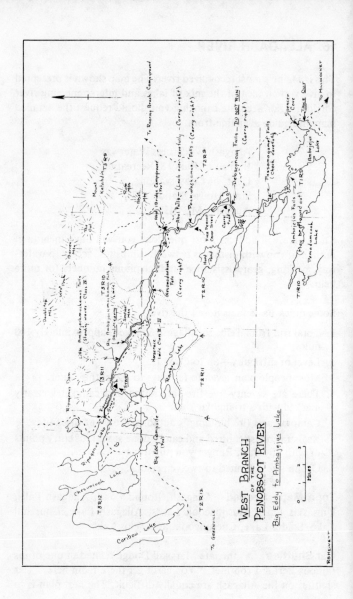

WEST BRANCH
OF THE
PENOBSCOT RIVER

Big Eddy to Ambajejus Lake

To Millinocket

Chase Out

Spencer Cove

Ambajejus Lake

Pamadumcook Lake

Passamagamet Falls (Check carefully) (Carry right)

Debsconeag Falls — DO NOT RUN — (Carry right)

T2 R9

Ambajejus Falls (hug bank/scout out) T1 R9

T1 R10

Rock wickaamus Falls — (Carry right)

Pine Falls (Look out—carefully) (Carry right)

Big Island Campground

To Roaring Brook Campground

Horse Race Rapids (Class III)

Carry Trail

Hurd Pond

Pockwockamus Falls (Carry right)

Nesowadnehunk Falls (Look out—carefully) (Carry right)

Abol Campground (Fee)

Abol Mtn

Rainbow Lake

T2 R10

T3 R10

Big Ambejackmockamus Falls (Boulder garden) Horserace Rapids—Class III—IV

Smart Mtn

Mount Katahdin

The Owl

Barren Mtn

Doubletop Mtn

Westor

Little Ambejackmockamus Falls (Steady waves—Class IV)

Ripogenus Dam

Ripogenus Lake

Staircase

Big Eddy Campsite (Fee)

Chesuncook Lake

Caribou Lake

T3 R11

T2 R11

T3 R12

T2 R12

To Greenville

0 1 2 3
MILES

R. S. HEWETT

have someone travel with you to Telos, drop you off, and drive home. Then, 10 days later, have them drive to Allagash Village and pick you up. Another plan would be for your shuttle people to drop you off, then return to Millinocket, Medway to I-95. Go north to Sherman Station, pick up Rt. 11 north to Fort Kent, then west on 161 to Allagash. Have them drop off your cars and return home in an extra vehicle.

Best Time to Canoe   Late May, June, July, August, Sept. (dam controlled).

17. WEST BRANCH OF PENOBSCOT
Big Eddy to Ambajejus

Powerful, deep, full of history, the Penobscot is a physically challenging river.

Starting Point   I-95 to Medway, Rt. 11/157 west to Millinocket, NW up the "Park Road" to Baxter State Park. Go past the entrance to the Park, cross the Penobscot at Abol Bridge. Twelve miles up this road, which parallels the river, is your launch site at Pray's Big Eddy Campsite.

Campsites   Pray's Big Eddy and Abol Campground are private sites, fee required. Fire permits are usually written for the lower river (foot of Pockwockamus Falls and head of Debsconeag Falls). Request permits from Maine Forest Service, Millinocket, ME 04622.

Car Shuttles   The shuttle here is easy. Simply leave a car at the "dike." See canoe map for Spencer Cove and take out.

Rapids & Carries   One mile below Pray's prepare for Class II ledge drop at Little Ambejackmockamus Falls. Run this right of center. The run below is through Class II, open rapids. Take out at foot of straight stretch of river. *Do not* go left around the corner for there lies Big Ambejackmockamus Falls! Under no cir-

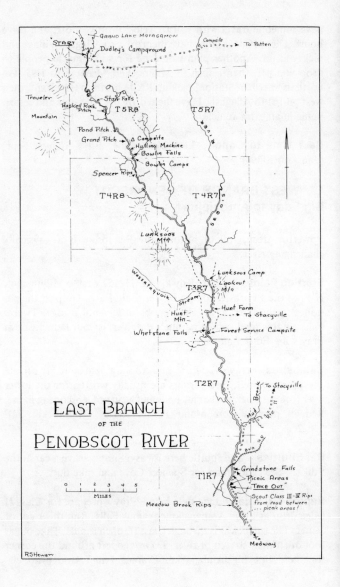

GRAND LAKE MATAGAMON

START

Dudley's Campground

Campsite → To Patten

Traveler

Mountain

Stair Falls

Haskell Rock Pitch

T5R8

T5R7

RIVER

Pond Pitch

Grand Pitch

△ Campsite

Hulling Machine

Bowlin Falls

Bowlin Camps

Spencer Rips

T4R8

T4R7

Seboeis

Lunksoos Mtn

Lunksoos Camp

Lookout Mtn

Wassataquoik Stream

T3R7

Hunt Farm → To Stacyville

Hunt Mtn

Whetstone Falls

Forest Service Campsite

T2R7

Mud Brook

Rte III

→ To Stacyville

EAST BRANCH
OF THE
PENOBSCOT RIVER

BMR

Grindstone Falls

Picnic Areas

"Take Out"

T1R7

Scout Class III-IV Rips
from road between
picnic areas!

Meadow Brook Rips

0 1 2 3 4 5
MILES

Medway

R.S.Hewen

cumstances should you run this—contains large "keepers" and several people have drowned here.

Class III rapids run all the way from below the carry to Nesowadnehunk Deadwater. This area can be a formidable place. Have some experienced people with you on this run. The deadwater is two miles long. Be prepared. Carry right to the road around Nesowadnehunk Falls (sharp vertical drop approx. 12′).

Mild Class II rapids run from here to Abol Falls. Both Abol & Pockwockamus must be carried on right bank. There is a road that parallels the river here which allows you to scout these quite easily. Be sure you do!

The Penobscot is free of rapids until Debsconeag Falls. Carry on the right bank at head of Falls 1/4 mile. Then 500 yards below the Falls run a sharp Class II ledge drop to flat river which runs with slow current until Passamagamet Falls. Scout these from island on left of center. In some water levels you may be able to run left of the island through heavy stacks—sharp Class III. The remainder of the paddle is through flowage and lakes to take out.

Best Time to Canoe   Early June through July.

18. EAST BRANCH PENOBSCOT

The East Branch is a big river, a profound river that flows south out of Grand Lake Matagamon. Wildlife is a key factor on this canoe trip—bring your camera.

Starting Point   I-95 to Medway, then Rt. 11 along the river to Grindstone and Stacyville. Turn left at Stacyville to Whetstone Falls. Leave your shuttle car here, then retrace to Stacyville and Sherman. Go north on Rt. 11 to Patten, left in Patten on 159 to Shin Pond, and ten miles further west to Matagamon's Wilderness Campground. Cross over the bridge, turn right along river to bank just below the dam.

Campsite Dudley's Matagamon Wilderness Campground right at the starting point is a private fee site. Fire permits are written for Haskell Rock, Pond Pitch, and Grand Pitch. Authorized sites exist for the lower river at Lunksoos Deadwater and Whetstone Falls. See canoe map. Request fire permits from Maine Forest Service, Island Falls, ME 04747.

Car Shuttle See comments under Starting Point.

Rapids & Carries The Penobscot flows over easy Class I rapids and current to Stair Falls. Run this Class II-III series of ledge drops in the center or line on right bank. The river has only a ruffled surface to Haskell Rock. Carry right—*do not* run Falls. Put in after 1/4 mile carry. Below Haskell watch for several sharp Class II stretches to Pond Pitch. Carry 300 yards on right bank. Easy going is the word all the way to Grand Pitch. Stay on left bank as you approach Pitch. Carry left 100 yards around this beautiful 20 foot waterfall. It is a short Class II run to Hulling Machine, a large waterfall. Carry left bank 1/4 mile and put in below the gorge. Sometimes the gorge below the main drop can be run. Scout it.

Bowlin Falls is really only a small ledge drop which is runnable. Rapids all the way to Lunksoos Deadwater are never more than Class I but you get a great ride.

Below Lunksoos there is an easy Class I rapid at Whetstone, your take out point. If you extend the trip to Grindstone the few rapids are all easy Class I. The one mile below Grindstone can be up to Class IV in medium water.

Best Time to Canoe Early June to early July.

19. MACHIAS RIVER

Starting Point There are several—From the Studd Mill Road just north of 1st Machias Lake, foot of 3rd Machias or, for a shortened trip, where Rt. 9 crosses the river at Airline Rapids.

Photo courtesy of Maine Fish & Game.

We'll take this from the most northerly point—foot of 3rd Lake. Use the Studd Mill Road to 1st Lake, cross over river, turn left (north). Drive on east side of river approximately 4½ miles, turn left to foot of old dam. Enter river here.

Campsites   There are no authorized sites. Fire permits must be obtained from District Forest Ranger, Wesley, ME 04686.

Car Shuttles   Drive from the bridge where Rt. 9 crosses the Machias to Junction of 192. Turn right on 192 to Northfield. Approximately one mile below Northfield, turn right on gravel road leading into a blueberry barren. Travel 1½ miles to Smith's Landing. Leave car here.

Rapids & Carries   In medium to high water you will encounter Class II rapids at Otter Falls & Long Falls which lie between 3rd and 2nd Lake. The river here is narrow so be ready for fast ride.

2nd Lake to 1st Lake—smooth current water to 1st Lake.

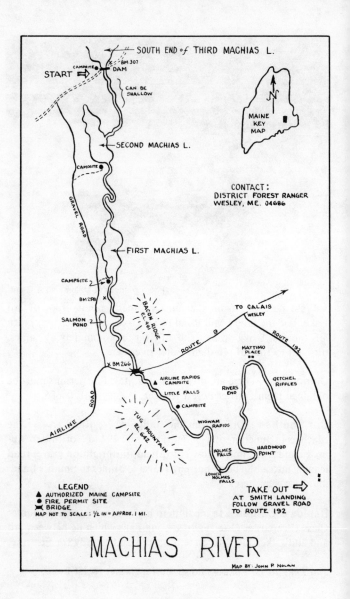

SOUTH END of THIRD MACHIAS L.

START

BM 307
CAMPSITE DAM

CAN BE SHALLOW

SECOND MACHIAS L.

CAMPSITE

CONTACT:
DISTRICT FOREST RANGER
WESLEY, ME. 04686

GRAVEL ROAD

FIRST MACHIAS L.

CAMPSITE

BM 258

SALMON POND

BACON RIDGE
EL. 461

TO CALAIS
WESLEY

ROUTE 9
ROUTE 192

MATTIMO PLACE

X BM 266

AIRLINE RAPIDS CAMPSITE

LITTLE FALLS

CAMPSITE

RIVER'S END

GETCHEL RIFFLES

TUG MOUNTAIN
EL. 642

WIGWAM RAPIDS

AIRLINE ROAD

HOLMES FALLS

HARDWOOD POINT

LOWER HOLMES FALLS

TAKE OUT
AT SMITH LANDING
FOLLOW GRAVEL ROAD
TO ROUTE 192

LEGEND
▲ AUTHORIZED MAINE CAMPSITE
● FIRE PERMIT SITE
✖ BRIDGE
MAP NOT TO SCALE : ½ IN = APPROX. 1 MI.

MAINE
KEY MAP

MACHIAS RIVER

MAP BY: JOHN P. NOLAN

42

1st Lake to Airline Rapids—intermittent, easy rapids for four miles. Watch for the S turn and entry to Carrick Pitch (sometimes written "Carrot" on topo maps.) Scout from right bank. This is sharp Class III with quick gradient. You may choose to carry (right bank). Below Carrick Pitch the West Branch enters and the river is full of fun Class I-II rapids to Rt. 9 and Airline Rapids.

Airline Rapids to Little Falls—Airline Rapids start just above the Rt. 9 bridge—these are Class II to III and can contain high standing waves that run for 1/2 mile. Very sporty spot but contains no sharp drop or falls.

In next four miles there are two Class II rapids, easily run. Wake up—we are at Little Falls.

Little Falls—this can be run in the right water level but contains sharp vertical ledges which can tear at canoes. Recommend lining at left bank. The Class II rapids below the falls is runnable.

The river flattens at Machias Eddy but sharpens up to Class II or III at the Wigwam Rapids. These are sharp and two miles long but again have no sudden drop or falls. Waves can be difficult in high water. Stop and scout from right bank. Three miles of dead water precede a logging bridge owned by St. Regis Paper Company just above Holmes Falls.

Holmes Falls—nasty, unrunnable, narrow gorge. Carry left just above bridge. Enter below falls. Watch carefully. Lower Holmes Falls is just around a right turn. These are runnable by experienced paddlers at the right water levels. Scout from one of the two islands.

Lower Holmes Falls to Smith's Landing—all flat or with some current. Take out at left bank at Smith's Landing.

Best Time to Canoe   Late April to third week in May.

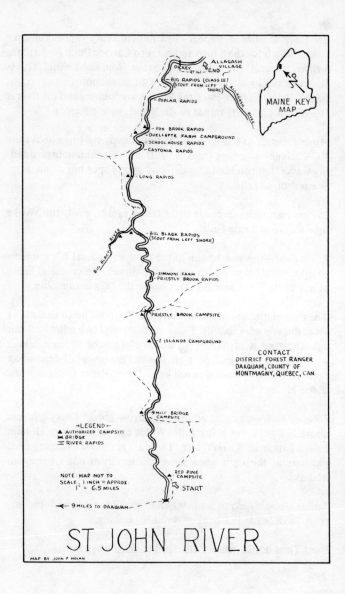

ALLAGASH VILLAGE

DICKEY RT 161

BIG RAPIDS (CLASS III)
(SCOUT FROM LEFT SHORE)

POPLAR RAPIDS

ALLAGASH RIVER

MAINE KEY MAP

FOX BROOK RAPIDS
OUELLSTTE FARM CAMPGROUND
SCHOOL HOUSE RAPIDS
CASTONIA RAPIDS

LONG RAPIDS

BIG BLACK RIVER

BIG BLACK RAPIDS
(SCOUT FROM LEFT SHORE)

SIMMONS FARM
PRIESTLY BROOK RAPIDS

PRIESTLY BROOK CAMPSITE

7 ISLANDS CAMPGROUND

CONTACT
DISTRICT FOREST RANGER
DAAQUAM, COUNTY OF
MONTMAGNY, QUÉBEC, CAN.

9 MILE BRIDGE
CAMPSITE

RED PINE
CAMPSITE

START

LEGEND
▲ AUTHORIZED CAMPSITE
✕ BRIDGE
≡ RIVER RAPIDS

NOTE: MAP NOT TO
SCALE. 1 INCH = APPROX
1" = 6.5 MILES

← 9 MILES TO DAAQUAM

ST JOHN RIVER

MAP BY JOHN P. NOLAN

20. ST. JOHN RIVER

Starting Points There are several. 5th St. John Pond, Baker Lake, or Red Pine Campsite. The point you choose will be decided by the length of time available and, most importantly, the amount of water. Baker Lake is probably the most popular start since float planes can easily transport you from Greenville. (see Bush Pilots.) The lower the water, the farther down river you start.

Campsites Request campsite material from North Maine Woods Association, Box 382, Ashland, ME 04732. (See Remote Campsites.)

There are good campsites all along the river. An excellent map is provided by North Maine Woods. Wood fires can be built only at their authorized sites. (See Remote Campsites.)

Car Shuttles The most convenient is to drive to Greenville, arrange air transportation to Baker Lake. Most air services can provide car shuttle to St. Francis from Greenville.

Driving is a bear. You must arrive at Baker Lake through Canada via Ste. Aurelie or through Daaquam to Red Pine Campsite. Great distances must be covered by any shuttle drivers. The best plan is flying!

Rapids & Carries Baker Lake to Baker Branch—the St. John is a forgiving, "teaching" river. Rapids from Baker Lake run for four miles easy Class I-II to Turner Brook followed by slow water to Baker Branch campsite.

Baker Branch to Southwest Branch—mixed slow water at the start coupled to rocky Class I-II rapids to junction of SW Branch of St. John.

SW Branch to NW Branch—river runs wide with mild rapids and fast current.

NW Branch to Nine Mile Bridge—at the junction of the NW Branch the river drops three levels through easy, rocky rapids (usually quite shallow in low water). The remainder of the paddle to Nine Mile is mild rapids through a wide, fast current river. (Don't look for the bridge, it was washed out in 1970. Only the abutments remain.

Nine Mile to Priestly Rapids—easy rapids, wide river, current to Seven Islands, more riffles to Priestly Rapids. A short, easy open rapid over the first drop, the second is not difficult but is often "scratchy", and a picking run through the rocks.

Priestly to Big Black Rapids—four miles of easy current, then two short Class I-II rapids. Now wake up! Big Black Rapids are the most difficult so far. Scout on left bank. River doglegs left and over a short ledge drop, sharp Class II complete with ledges and large rocks followed by gradual rapids (Class II) to a second easier set. Run the first drop right of center.

Big Black to Big Rapids—all the rapids in this section are easy, open Class I-II fun and relaxing.

Big Rapids—a full two miles in length. Continuous up to Class III where river doglegs left. These are forceful, most difficult of trip, can have large standing waves. In low water the waves are still high, plus huge boulders crop up!

This is generally a runnable set at most water levels. If you feel uncomfortable carry left on the road that parallels the river. Very "sporty spot." Great way to end a canoe trip!

Best Time to Canoe   Late May to mid-June (water level drops rapidly—check out).

2 Canoe Rentals

Now think about it. Don't you get just a drop of apprehension when your neighbor slides over and asks to borrow your canoe? The businesses listed below have to have lots of pluck—or maybe it's luck. At any rate you can come to Maine without your canoe beaked over and webbed down all over your car. Drop these folks a line in advance and a canoe will be here waiting for you!

Canoe Rental Businesses

Allagash Wilderness Outfitters
Box 620S, Star Route 76, Greenville, ME 04441

Canal Bridge Canoes
Route 302, Fryeburg, ME 04037

Great Pond Marina
Route 27, Belgrade, ME 04917

Indian Cellar Canoe Rental
Route 202, Hollis, ME 04042

Katahdin Outfitters
P.O. Box 34, Millinocket, ME 04462

Kennebec Canoe Rental Sales
25 School St., Augusta, ME 04330

Maine Canoe Adventure
Box 105, Route 161, Allagash, ME 04774

Maine Wilderness Canoe Basin
Off Route 6, Springfield, ME 04487

North Country Outfitters
Waterford Rd., Box 181, North Bridgton, ME 04057

North Country Outfitters
P.O. Box 81-M, Rockwood, ME 04478

Canoe Rental Businesses (*cont'd*)

Northern Outdoors
Route 201, The Forks, ME 04985

Outdoor Connection
Long Lake, Box 1265 MCD, Jackman, ME 04945

Pelletier's Campground
P.O. Box 8, St. Francis, ME 04774

Pemaquid River Canoe Rental, Inc.
P.O. Box 46, Bristol, ME 04539

River Run Canoe Rental
Rt. 160, Brownfield, ME 04010

Saco Bound/Northern Waters
Route 302, Saco River, Center Conway, NH
P.O. Box, Fryeburg, ME 04037

Saco River Canoe & Kayak
Box 111, Route 5 North, Fryeburg, ME 04037

Sally Mountain Cabins
SR 64, Box 50, Jackman, ME 04945

Sauer's
Box 989, Millinocket, ME 04462

Sunrise County Canoe Expedition (outfitter)
Cathance Lake, Grove P.O. ME 04368

Webb's Wilderness Outfitters
West Forks, ME 04985

Mike Carrol photo.

3 Equipment Dealers

The companies listed below enjoy an excellent reputation for quality canoeing equipment. A postcard directed to these distributors will result in an excellent selection of paddles (straight and bent), PFD's, waterproof bags, canoes and inflatables, poles, knee pads, car top carriers, and tents.

Maine

Kittery Trading Post Rt. 1, Kittery, ME 63904, Tel. (207) 439-2700

L.L. Bean's Freeport, ME 04033, Tel. 1-800-221-4221

Moss Tent Works Mt. Battie Road, Camden, ME 04843, Tel. (207) 236-8368

Northeastern Canoe Paddles River Road, Calais, ME 04619, Tel. (207) 454-2667

Old Town Canoe Old Town, ME 04468, Tel. (207) 827-5513

National

Alumacraft Boat Co. 315 W. St. Julien, St. Peter, MN 56082

Aqua Bag Box 328, Anstead, WV 25812

Bart Hauthaway 640 Boston Post Rd., Weston, MA 02193

Blue Hole Canoes Company P.O. Box 179, Sunbright, TN 37872

Camp-ways, Inc. 12915 So. Springs St., Los Angeles, CA 90061

Chicagoland Canoe Basin, Inc. 4019 N. Narragansett Avenue, Chicago, IL 60634

Coleman Canoe Company, Inc. 250 N. St. Francis, Wichita, KS 67201

Dry Box, Inc. 1911 Laurel Springs Lane, Humble, TX 77338

Eastern Mt. Sports Vose Farm Rd., Peterborough, NH 03458

Gillespie Paddles 139 Kamer St., Rochester, NY 14634

Grade VI Expedition Outfitters P.O. Box 8, Urbana, IL 61801

Great Canadian 45 Water St. (Off I-290), Worcester, MA 01604

Great World, Inc. 250 Farms Village Rd., West Simsbury, CT 06092

Grey Owl Paddles 101 Sheldon Dr., Cambridge, Ontario, NIR 6T6 Canada

Grumman Boats Marathon, NY 13803

Hidde Paddles Rt. 3, Elk River, MN 55330

Jenson Canoe Co. 308 78th Ave., No. Minneapolis, MN 55444

McCann Paddles 200 Main St., Cornwell, WI 54732

Michi Craft Corp. 20,000 Nineteen Mile Rd., Big Rapids, MI 49307

Mohawk Canoes P.O. Box 668, Dept. 6C, Longwood, FL 32750

Mad River Canoes, Inc. P.O. Box 610, Waitsfield, VT 05673

Northwest River Supplies P.O. Box 9186 C1, Moscow, ID 83843

Omega 266 Border St., E. Boston, MA 02128

Pacific Water Sports 16205 Pacific Highway S., Seattle, WA 98188

Phoenix Products, Inc. U.S. Rt. 421, Tyner, KY 40486

Robco Box 216, Tyner, KY 40486

Sawyer Canoe Co. 234 State St., Oscoda, MI 48750

Sea Eagle Dept. C3B, St. James, NY 11780

Sierra Designs 247 Fourth St., Oakland, CA 94801

Smokercraft, Inc. P.O. Box 65, New Paris, IN 46553

Stearns P.O. Box 1498, St. Cloud, MI 56302

Voyageur's Ltd. P.O. Box 512, Gardiner, KS 66030

Wayfarer Expeditions, Inc. 1303 College St., Springfield, MO 65806

■ Water Adventures

4 Outfitters

Each of the outfitters below will provide all the heavy equipment (canoes, tents, etc.). You will need all your own personal gear (sleeping bags, rain gear, etc.). Most provide excellent brochures describing their services. Rivers generally run are the Allagash, St. John, West Branch Penobscot, Saco, Moose, and St. Croix rivers.

Grab a paddle, forget all your cares. Come paddle a "hundred miles and look at something." The outfitters below will take all the work and worry out of the trip.

Allagash Canoe Trips   Dana Shaw, 6 Winchester Street, Presque Isle, ME 04769, Tel. (207) 764-0494

Allagash Guide, Inc.   Blaine Miller, Box 703, Route #1, Norridgewock, ME 04957, Tel. (207) 696-3919 or 634-3253

Allagash Outfitters   Wilmer Hafford, Box 149, Allagash, ME 04774, Tel. (207) 398-3277

Allagash River Canoeing   Ken York, Gen'l Delivery, Bucksport, ME 04416, Tel. (207) 469-7151

Allagash River Trips   Fred King, Route #5, Box 98, 16 Woodside Road, Augusta, ME 04330, Tel. (207) 623-4429

Allagash Sporting Camps   Bob & Lois O'Leary, Box 169A, Allagash, ME 04774, Tel. (207) 398-3555

Allagash Wilderness Outfitters   Dick & Judy Givens, May 1–Nov. 30, Box 620, Star Route 76, Greenville, ME 04441, Radio contact 207-695-2821, Dec. 1–April 30

Big Machias Lake Camps   Ivan R. Porter, P.O. Box 327, Ashland, ME 04732, Tel. (207) 435-6977

Caribou Outfitters (Allagash River Trips)   Frank Connolly, Route #1, Box 40, Caribou, ME 04376, Tel. (207) 498-3247

Gardner's Sporting Camps Box 127, Allagash, ME 04774, Tel. (207) 398-3168

Gilpatrick's Guide Service Gil Gilpatrick, RFD #1, Box 1003, Fairfield, ME 04937, Tel. (207) 453-6959

Guided Maine Wilderness Canoe Trips Fred Westerberg, Box 111, Fryeburg, ME 04037, Tel. (207) 453-6959

Jalbert's Allagash Camps Greg Jalbert, P.O. Box 28, Fort Kent, ME 04794, Tel. (207) 444-5928 or 834-5015

Katahdin Outfitters Don Hibbs, P.O. Box 34, Millinocket, ME 04462, Tel. (207) 723-5700

Libby Camps Matt & Ellen Libby, Props., Box 145, Masardis, ME 04759, Tel. (207) 435-4202 or 435-6233

Lutes, David Box 232, Allagash, ME 04774, Tel. (207) 398-3275

Maine Canoe Adventures Cross Rock Canoe Landing, RFD #1, Box 105, St. Francis, ME 04774, Tel. (207) 398-3259 or 398-3191

McBreairty, Chester Allagash, ME 04774, Tel. (207) 398-3197

Moosehead Country Outfitters P.O. Box D, Greenville, ME 04441, Tel. (207) 695-2272

North Country Outfitters (operating out of *The Birches*), P.O. Box 81, Rockwood, ME 04478, Tel. (207) 534-2242 or 534-7305

Northern River Runners Eric & Elaine Hendrickson, RFD #2, Box 383, Presque Isle, ME 04769, Tel. (207) 455-4069

Northwest Outfitters Arlo Caron, Box 216, Allagash, ME 04774, Tel. (207) 398-3573

North Woods Ways Garrett & Alexandria Conover, RFD #3, Box 87A, Dover Foxcroft, ME 04426 (has snow camping special)

Pelletier, Edwin P.O. Box 8, St. Francis, ME 04774, Tel. (207) 398-3187

Scotty's Flying Service Box 256, Shin Pond, ME 04765, Tel. (207) 528-2626 or 528-2528

Sunrise County Canoe Expeditions Cathance Lake, Grove P.O., ME 04368, Tel. (207) 454-7708

Taiga Outfitters Bob Johnson, RFD #1, Box 147B, Ashland, ME 04732, Tel. (207) 435-6851

5 Rafting Expeditions

Rafting is a dynamite sport in Maine. Both the West Branch of the Penobscot and the Kennebec Gorge provide all the action a red-blooded person needs. In fact, I'll lean way over the gunwale to state that if you go rafting in Maine you will have a fantastic time. It *is* an adventure. Most companies provide riverside lunch of "steak & good stuff." Names of exciting spots on the river will stick in your memory. *On the Kennebec:* Rockgarden, Sluiceway, Sisters, the Alleyway, Z turn, Magic Falls. *On the Penobscot:* Rip gorge, Troublemaker, Cribwork, Big Ambejackmockamus.

There are approximately fifteen rafters running on the rivers. Some have a keen understanding of the need to cooperate with the power companies which control the water flow, others do not.

I will only recommend to you those which adhere to a strict code of friendliness and compatability with each other and the river. These all belong to the Whitewater Outfitters Association of Maine, Inc. They are listed in alphabetical order, but Hockmeyer, Ernst, and Hoddinott were the pioneers.

Downeast, Inc.
The Forks, ME 04985

Rick Hoddinott
Tel. (207) 663–2281

Maine Whitewater, Inc.
Bingham, ME 04920

Jim Ernst
Tel. (207) 672–4814

**New England Whitewater
  Center**
The Forks, ME 04985

Joe Bruce,
Matt Polstein
Tel. (207) 663–4455

Northern Whitewater Expeditions, Inc.	Wayne Hockmeyer
P.O. Box 100	Tel. (207) 663–2271
The Forks, ME 04985	

Northern Whitewater
Expeditions, Inc.
P.O. Box 100
The Forks, ME 04985

Wayne Hockmeyer
Tel. (207) 663–2271

Unicorn Rafting
Expeditions, Inc.
West Forks, ME 04985

Jay Schurman
Tel. (207) 663–2258

Wilderness Rafting
Expeditions
Rockwood, ME 04478

Dave Babb
Tel. (207) 534–7328
John Willard
Tel. (207) 534–7305

Wildwater Adventures
RFD #3, Box 7860
Skowhegan, ME 04976

Dave Sargent
Tel. (207) 474–2251

Each rafting outfitter has slightly different costs, but a fair guess of the average is $70–80.00 for a one-day raft trip. Wet suits can be rented from $5.00 for top only to $12.00 for a full suit.

These are nice people with experienced, trained river guides. Plan a raft trip. You'll be glad you did!

6 Windjammer Cruises

Windjammer cruises offer a chance to break away from the fast pace of life. A cruise along the Maine Coast is a salty, refreshing experience—with no horns blowing!

Schooner *Adventure* Capt. Jim Sharp, Box 696A, Camden, ME 04843, Tel. (207) 236-4449

Ketch *Cygnet*   Cygnet Charters—Marshall Bolster, Jr., RFD #1, Lincolnville, ME 04849, Tel. (207) 763-3642

Schooner *Day Spring*   Capt. Bill & Judy Wasson, P.O.Box 6110, Camden, ME 04843, Tel. (207) 236-8374

Schooner *Flying Fish*   Capt. Earl MacKensie, Box 41B, Islesboro, ME 04848, Tel. (207) 734-6984

Schooner *Heritage*   Capts. Lee & Foss, Box 482D, Rockland, ME 04814, Tel. (207) 594-8007

Schooner *Isaac H. Evans*   Capts. Lee & Foss, Box 482D, Rockland, ME 04814, Tel. (207) 594-8007

Schooner *Janet May*   Capt. Steven Pagels, 129 Stillwater Rd., Cherryfield, ME 04622, Tel. (207) 546-7532

Schooner *Lewis R. French*   Capts. Lee & Foss, Box 482D, Rockland, ME 04814, Tel. (207) 594-8007

Schooner *Mattie*   Capt. Les Bex, Maine Windjammer Cruises, Inc. Box 617DE, Camden, ME 04843, Tel. (207) 236-2938

Schooner *Mercantile*   Capt. Les Bex, Maine Windjammer Cruises, Inc. Box 617DE, Camden, ME 04843, Tel. (207) 236-2938

Schooner *Mistress*   Capt. Les Bex, Maine Windjammer Cruises, Inc. Box 617DE, Camden, ME 04843, Tel. (207) 236-2938

Windjammer *Nathaniel Bowditch*   Capt. Gib Philbrick, Box D, Harborside, ME 04642, Tel. (207) 326-4822

Schooner *Roseway*   Capt. Jim Sharp, Box 696A, Camden, ME 04843, Tel. (207) 236-4449

Schooner *Stephen Taber*   70 Elm St., Drawer C, Camden, ME 04843, Tel. (207) 236-3520

Schooner *Timberwind*   Capt. Bill Alexander, Box 2470, Rockport, ME 04856, Tel. (207) 236-9063 or 763-3137

Schooner *Victory Chimes*   Capt. Frederick B. Guild, Box 368DE, Rockland, ME 04841, Tel. (207) 596-6060 or 326-8856

Cruising Trimaran *Wind Dance*   Capts. Peter & Anita Sandefur, *Summer:* P.O. Box 596, Boothbay Harbor, ME 04538, Tel. (207) 633-2284 *Winter:* P.O. Box 2211, Stuart, FL 33498

Each sailing ship captain will provide you with a complete brochure upon request.

7 Charter Boats

Happy Hooker, Devil's Den, Buccaneer, Mystery. Now those names just have to tickle your imagination and are just a sampling of Maine's charter boats offering you a chance to encounter cod, mackerel, halibut, and shark. Seals, osprey, and large flocks of sea ducks are always part of this great Maine adventure.

The following is as complete a list as can be found. *Boats are listed from southwest to northeast along the Maine coast.* All provide deep sea fishing. Some specialize in shark, and a number also provide scenic island cruises and seal watching. The season for most captains is May to October. Write to the Captain and he will mail rates, etc.

York Harbor

E-Z, Dan Donnell Dock, York Harbor, ME 03911
 Tel. (207) 363–5634
Elizabeth Ann, York Harbor, ME 03911
 Tel. (207) 363–6247
Porpoise III, Cider Hill Road, York Harbor, ME 03911
 Tel. (207) 363–5106

York

Rambler II, Sewall's Bridge, York, ME 03909
 Tel. (207) 363–3127

Ogunquit

The Bonny Clark, Box 837, Ogunquit, ME 03907
Ruth Bee, Post Road, Ogunquit, ME 03907
 Tel. (207) 646–2257
Sea Hawk, P.O. Box 401, Ogunquit, ME 03907
 Tel. (207) 646–7222

Ugly Ann, Perkins Cove, Ogunquit, ME 03907
   Tel. (207) 646-7207

Kennebunk

Deep Water, P.O. Box 142, Kennebunk, ME 04045
   Tel. (207) 985-2286

Kennebunkport

Capt. Pete's, Box 468, Kennebunkport, ME 04046
Indian, Box 746, Kennebunk, ME 04045
   Tel. (207) 967-5912
Sonnie W., Box 468, Kennebunkport, ME 04046
   Tel. (207) 985-3893

Biddeford

Mary C., 521 Pool Road, Biddeford, ME 04005
   Tel. (207) 284-4950

Scarborough

Pegasus, Scarborough, ME 04074
   Tel. (207) 883-6011
San R. Marie, 74 East Grand Ave., Scarborough, ME 04074
   Tel. (207) 883-5002

Portland

Abenaki, Portland, ME 04101
   Tel. (207) 774-7871
Anjin-San Charters, 210 Prospect St., Portland, ME 04103
Christopher, P.O. Box 1255, Portland, ME 04103
   Tel. (207) 883-5710
Devil's Den, P.O. Box 272, Scarborough, ME 04074
   Tel. (207) 883-9661
Indian II, Old Port Mariner Fleet, Box 1084, Portland, ME 04103
   Tel. (207) 642-3270
Lazy Day, 128 Brentwood St., Portland, ME 04103
   Tel. (207) 774-0122

Venturer, Old Port Mariner Fleet, Box 1084, Portland, ME 04103
  Tel. (207) 642-3270

Bailey Island

Kristy K, 170 Commercial St., Portland, ME 04103
  Tel. (207) 774-6498 or 846-9592
Odyssey II, Dockside Marina, Bailey Island, ME 04003
  Tel. (207) 833-6656
Strike, Steward Place, Dockside Marina, Bailey Island, ME 04003
  Tel. (207) 833-6656

South Harpswell

Happy Hooker, Rt. 123, So. Harpswell, ME 04079
  Tel. (207) 833-5447

West Point

Hazel A., Georgetown, ME 04548

Small Point

Yankee, Hermit Island Inc., Small Point, ME 04567
  Tel. (207) 443-2101

Boothbay Harbor

Argo, Boothbay Harbor, ME 04538
Backlash, 89 Grove St., Augusta, ME 04330
Buccaneer, Boothbay Harbor, ME 04538
Capella, Middle Road, Boothbay Harbor, ME 04538
  Tel. (207) 633-3562
Capt. Fish, Pier 1, Boothbay Harbor, ME 04538
Connoisseur, Boothbay Harbor, ME 04538
  Tel. (207) 633-6244
Fish Hawk, Pier 3, Boothbay Harbor, ME 04538
  Tel. (207) 633-3244
Gertrude "R," Box 133, Boothbay Harbor, ME 04538
  Tel. (207) 882-7160
Godfather, P.O. Box 612, Boothbay Harbor, ME 04538
  Tel. (207) 633-6327

Goodtime Excursions, Boothbay Harbor, ME 04538
   Tel. (207) 633-3244

Island Cruises to Monhegan, P.O. Box 102, Boothbay Harbor,
   ME 04538

Linekin II, Boothbay Harbor, ME 04538
   Tel. (207) 633-4925

Mystery, Boothbay Harbor, ME 04538
   Tel. (207) 633-3244 or 633-2626

Sea Hag, Park St., Boothbay Harbor, ME 04538
   Tel. (207) 633-3844

Shark II, Boothbay Harbor, ME 04538
   Tel. (207) 633-4598

Squalus Charters, Brown Bros. Wharf, Boothbay Harbor, ME
   04538
   Tel. (207) 445-4132

Spruce Head

Dolphin, Spruce Head, ME 04859
   Tel. (207) 594-9362

Rockland

Henrietta, Spruce Island, ME 04859
   Tel. (207) 594-5411

Mt. Katahdin, P.O. Box 1112, Rockland, ME 04841
   Tel. (207) 584-8115

Stonington

Palmer Day II, Stonington, ME 04681
   Tel. (207) 367-2207

Sedgwick

Nancy Lee, Sargentville, ME 04673
   Tel. (207) 359-4445

Bar Harbor

Cod Fish, Bar Harbor Town Port, Bar Harbor, ME 04609
   Tel. (207) 288-3889

Dolphin, West St., Bar Harbor, ME 04609
   Tel. (207) 288-5741

Osprey, West St., Bar Harbor, ME 04609
   Tel. (207) 288-5741

Seal Harbor

Sea Wind, Seal Harbor, ME 04675
   Tel. (207) 276-3980

Seal, Seal Harbor, ME 04675
   Tel. (207) 276-3980

Jonesport

Chief, Jonesport, ME 04649
   Tel. (207) 497-5933

Eastport

Quoddy Dam, Eastport, ME 04631
   Tel. (207) 853-4303

Maine State Development Office photo.

8 Ocean Beaches

If you have a hankering to wiggle your toes in good old Maine sand, these beaches will give you a chance. If bathing facilities such as bathhouses, toilets, snack bars are available they will be noted. Bring the kids, throw in a bucket and shovel—build a sand castle in Maine!

Note: Beaches are listed North to South.	Map Key	Restrooms	Showers	Fee (Approx.)	Time Open	Open all year	Parking	Snack Bars
Roque Bluffs Roque Bluffs	E-9	x			8:00	May-Sept.	Moderate	
Sand Mt. Desert	D-7	x			Dawn	June-Sept.	Moderate	x
Lamoine Lamoine	D-7				8:00	Yes	Moderate	
Sandy Point Stockton Springs	D-6					x	Large	
Birch Point Rockland	D-5	x			9:00	May-Sept.	Limited	

Note: Beaches are listed North to South.	Map Key	Restrooms	Showers	Fee (Approx.)	Time Open	Open all year	Parking	Snack Bars
Crescent Owls Head	C-5	×			Dawn	×	Limited	
Half Mile Georgetown	C-3	×	Dress. Rms.	$1.50	9:00	June-Sept.	Ample	×
Mile Georgetown	C-3	×	Dress. Rms.	$1.50	9:00	Yes	Limited	×
Reid State Park Georgetown	C-3	×	×	$2.00 per car	9:00 to sunset	Yes	Large	×
Popham Phippsburg	C-3	×		$2.00 per car	9:00 to sunset	May 1 to Sept 30	Moderate	
Head Phippsburg	C-3	×		$2.00	9:00	May-Sept.	Moderate	×
Thomas Point Brunswick	C-3	×	×	$1.50	9:00	May-Sept.	Large	×
Willard So. Portland	B-2	×			9:00	×	Moderate	×
Crescent Cape Elizabeth	B-2	×	×	$2.00	9:00	May-Sept.	Ample	×

Beach	Town	Map			Fee/Parking	Open	Lifeguard	Size	Facilities
Ferry	Scarborough	B-2	x		$2.00 Parking	Dawn	Yes	Moderate	x
Grand	Scarborough	B-2			Parking	Dawn	Yes	Moderate	x
Higgins	Scarborough	B-2			Parking	Dawn	Yes	Moderate	Close by
Scarborough	Scarborough	B-2	x		Parking	Dawn	x	Moderate	x
Western	Scarborough	B-2	x		$2.00 Parking	8:00	x	Moderate	x
Old Orchard	Old Orchard	B-2	x	x		Dawn	x	Large	x
Fortunes Rocks	Biddeford	B-2				9:00	Yes	Limited	
Gooch's	Kennebunk	B-2					Seasonal	Limited	
Wells	Wells	B-2	x		$2.00 Parking	8:00	x	Moderate	x
Ogunquit	Ogunquit	A-1	x	x	$5.00 per car	Dawn	x	Limited	x
Long	York	A-1			Metered parking	Dawn	Yes	Moderate	x
Short Sand	York	A-1	x			7:00	x	Moderate	x

■ Boating

9 Boating Regulations

Just some quick words before you launch your watercraft.
Maine has some regulations worth noting.

1. Registration Any boat powered by any type of motor
or over sixteen feet in length must be registered. Maine
registration is for 2 years at a fee of $6.00. If you are from
out of state and your boat is legally registered in your home
state (except N.H.) you may use your boat in Maine for
sixty consecutive days without a Maine registration. If your
boat is not registered in your home state, you must obtain a
Maine registration through the Dept. of Inland Fisheries &
Wildlife, 284 State St., Augusta, ME 04330. Registration
regulations for both salt and fresh water craft are the same.

2. Town Excise Tax If your boat is in Maine for more
than 75 days you must obtain stickers for your boat (or any
watercraft using a motor) from the town office in which
your watercraft is principally moored or docked. If you are
here less than 75 days you need to go to the town office and
fill out an exemption form showing you will not have your
boat here for 75 days.

3. Who may operate Children under twelve may not
operate a motorboat of more than 10 horsepower unless
under the immediate supervision of someone sixteen or
older.

4. Water skiing (a.) requires a U.S. Coast Guard approved personal flotation device (PFD), and (b.) must have an observer in addition to the driver in the boat.

5. All boats regardless of type must have one PFD for each person aboard.

6. Night Operation All boats must show red and green at the bow and a white stern light visible 360°.

Now armed with all this data you can grin at the next warden who comes cruising up asking to see your PFD's!

---

10 Boat Launches

STATE SPONSORED AND ASSISTED
BOAT LAUNCHING SITES

*CW = Both cold and warm water fisheries C = Cold water fisheries only W = Warm water fisheries only T = Tidal	Fisheries*	Carry In Launch	Canoe Launch	All Tide Ramp	Fee	Map Index
Town — **Water Body**						
Acton — Great East Lake	W					B-1
Acton — Horn Pond	W					B-1
Addison — Pleasant River	T			•		E-8
Auburn — Lake Auburn	CW					D-2
Augusta — Kennebec River	T			•		D-3

*CW = Both cold and warm water fisheries C = Cold water fisheries only W = Warm water fisheries only T = Tidal	Fisheries*	Carry In Launch	Canoe Launch	All Tide Ramp	Fee	Map Index
Town	**Water Body**					
Baileyville	St. Croix River	CW					F-9
Baldwin	Sand Pond	CW					C-1
Bar Harbor	Frenchman Bay	T			•		D-7
Bath	Kennebec River	T			•		C-3
Beaver Cove Plt.	Moosehead Lake	C				•	G-4
Belgrade	Great Pond	CW					D-3
Belgrade	Messalonskee Lake	CW					E-3
Biddeford	Saco River	T			•		B-2
Biddeford	Saco River	W					B-2
Boothbay	Linekin Bay	T					C-4
Bowdoinham	Cathance River	T			•		C-3
Bridgton	Long Lake	CW					C-1
Bristol	Pemaquid River	T			•		C-4
Brownfield	Saco River	W	•				C-1
Brunswick	Buttermilk Cove	T					C-3
Brunswick	New Meadows River	T			•		C-3
Brunswick	Middle Bay	T			•		C-3

*CW = Both cold and warm water fisheries C = Cold water fisheries only W = Warm water fisheries only T = Tidal		Fisheries*	Carry In Launch	Canoe Launch	All Tide Ramp	Fee	Map Index
Town	**Water Body**						
Casco	Sebago Lake	CW				•	C-2
Chelsea	Kennebec River	T					D-3
Cherryfield	Narraguagus River	T					E-8
Cherryfield	Narraguagus River	C					E-8
Chesterville	Egypt Pond	C	•				E-3
Damariscotta	Damariscotta River	T			•		C-4
Danforth	Baskahegan Stream	W					G-8
Danforth	Grand Lake	CW					G-8
Denmark	Hancock	CW					D-1
Dover-Foxcroft	Sebec Lake	CW					F-5
Eagle Lake	Eagle Lake	C					K-6
Eastbrook	Molasses Pond	CW					E-7
East Machias	Gardner Lake	CW					E-9
Edmunds Twp.	Cobscook Bay	T			•	•	E-10
Eliot	Piscataqua River	T			•		A-1
Ellsworth	Graham Lake	W					E-7

*CW = Both cold and warm water fisheries C = Cold water fisheries only W = Warm water fisheries only T = Tidal	Fisheries*	Carry In Launch	Canoe Launch	All Tide Ramp	Fee	Map Index
Town **Water Body**						
Ellsworth	Green Lake	CW					E-7
Ellsworth	Union River	T			•		E-7
Embden	Embden Pond	CW					F-3
Enfield	Cold Stream Pond	C					F-6
Falmouth	Highland Lake	CW	•				C-2
Fayette	Tilton Pond	W	•				D-3
Fort Kent	Black Lake	C					K-6
Franklin	Georges Pond	W					E-7
Fryeburg	Lovewell Pond	W					C-1
Fryeburg	Saco River	CW		•			C-1
Gardiner	Kennebec River	T			•		D-3
Glenwood Plt.	Wytopitlock Lake	W					H-7
Greenville	Moosehead Lake	CW					G-4
Greenwood	South Pond	CW					D-1
Hallowell	Kennebec River	T			•		D-3
Hartland	Great Moose Lake	CW					E-4
Hope	Alford Lake	CW				•	D-5
Jonesport	Chandler Bay	T			•		E-9

*CW = Both cold and warm water fisheries only C = Cold water fisheries only W = Warm water fisheries only T = Tidal	Fisheries*	Carry In Launch	Canoe Launch	All Tide Ramp	Fee	Map Index
Town **Water Body**						
Kenduskeag Kenduskeag Stream	W					F-5
Lamoine Frenchman Bay	T			•		D-7
Lamoine Frenchman Bay	T			•	•	D-7
Liberty Lake St. George	CW				•	D-5
Limestone Trafton Lake	C					J-8
Lincoln Long Pond	W					G-6
Lincoln Mattanawcook Lake	W					G-6
Lincoln Penobscot River	W					G-6
Lincoln Plt. Aziscohos Lake	C					F-1
Linneus Nickerson Lake	C					H-8
Litchfield Buker Pond	CW					D-3
Litchfield Woodbury Pond	CW					D-3
Lubec Johnson Bay	T				•	E-10
Madison Wesserunsett Lake	CW					E-3
Medway Penobscot River	W					G-6
Milbridge Narraguagus River	T					E-8

*CW = Both cold and warm water fisheries C = Cold water fisheries only W = Warm water fisheries only T = Tidal	Fisheries*	Carry In Launch	Canoe Launch	All Tide Ramp	Fee	Map Index
Town **Water Body**						
Monmouth Cobbosseecontee Lake	CW					D-3
Monmouth Cochnewagon Lake	CW					D-3
Monmouth Wilson Pond	CW					D-3
Mt. Vernon Echo Lake	CW					E-3
Mt. Vernon Long Pond	CW					E-3
Mt. Vernon Taylor Pond	W					E-3
New Limerick Drews Lake	C					H-8
Newport Sebasticook Lake	W					E-5
Norridgewock Kennebec River	W					E-3
Norway Pennesseewassee Lake	CW					D-2
Orland Toddy Pond	CW					E-6
Orono Pushaw Lake	W					E-6
Palermo Sheepscot Pond	CW					D-4
Penobscot No. Bay & Baga-duce River	T					D-6
Perry Passamaquoddy Bay	T			•		F-10

*CW = Both cold and warm water fisheries C = Cold water fisheries only W = Warm water fisheries only T = Tidal		Fisheries*	Carry In Launch	Canoe Launch	All Tide Ramp	Fee	Map Index
Town	**Water Body**						
Poland	Lower Range Pond	W				•	C-2
Portage	Portage Lake	C					J-7
Portland	Casco Bay	T			•		C-2
Presque Isle	Arnold Brook Lake	C					J-8
Presque Isle	Echo Lake	C				•	J-8
Presque Isle	Presque Isle Stream	C					J-8
Princeton	Lewy Lake	W					F-9
Rangeley	Rangeley Lake	C				•	F-1
Rangeley	Rangeley Lake (Oquossoc)	C					F-1
Rangeley	Rangeley Lake (Town Park)	C					F-1
Readfield	Maranacook Lake	CW					D-3
Readfield	Torsey Pond	W					D-3
Richmond	Kennebec River	T			•		D-3
Robbinston	St. Croix River	T			•		F-10
Rockland	Rockland Harbor	T			•		D-5

*CW = Both cold and warm water fisheries C = Cold water fisheries only W = Warm water fisheries only T = Tidal		Fisheries*	Carry In Launch	Canoe Launch	All Tide Ramp	Fee	Map Index
Town	**Water Body**						
Rockport	Rockport Harbor	T			•	•	D-5
Sabattus	Sabattus Pond	W					D-3
Sangerville	Center Pond	CW					F-4
St. Agatha	Long Lake	C					K-7
St. George	Port Clyde	T			•		C-5
St. George	Tenants Harbor	T			•		C-5
Scarborough	Nonesuch River	T					B-2
Searsmont	Quantabacook Pond	W					D-5
Searsport	Searsport Harbor	T			•		D-5
Skowhegan	Kennebec River	W					E-4
Smithfield	North Pond	W					E-3
So. Orrington	Penobscot River	T			•		E-6
So. Portland	Fore River	T			•		B-2
Stockholm	Little Madawaska River	C	•				K-7
Stockton Springs	Stockton Harbor	T			•		D-6
Swans Island	Jericho Bay	T			•		D-7
Township "C"	Richardson Lake	C					E-1

72

*CW = Both cold and warm water fisheries C = Cold water fisheries only W = Warm water fisheries only T = Tidal		Fisheries*	Carry In Launch	Canoe Launch	All Tide Ramp	Fee	Map Index
Town	**Water Body**						
TIR9	Ambajejus Lake	CW					G-6
T16-R4	Madawaska Lake	CW					K-7
Union	Seven Tree Pond	W					D-5
Vanceboro	Spednik Lake	CW					G-9
Vassalboro	Three Mile Pond	CW					D-4
Verona	Penobscot River	T			•		E-6
Vinalhaven	Isle Au Haut Bay	T			•		C-6
Waterboro	Little Ossipee Pond	CW					B-1
Weld	Webb Lake	CW				•	E-2
West Paris	Moose Pond	W					D-2
Westport Island	Sheepscot River	T			•		C-4
Wilton	Wilson Lake	CW					E-2
Winthrop	Maranacook Lake	CW					D-3
Woodstock	Bryant Pond	C					D-1

11 Boat Yards/Marinas

My father owned a boat yard back in the good old days. In case you are of the more recent vintage of fiberglass and Kevlar, that was a time when you scrambled for the shady side of some hulking beached monster of a watercraft and scrubbed seaweed and barnacles off the hull with a wire brush. Copper bronze and red copper were in as bottom paints along with caulking and puttying garboard planks. Stems were hewn with an adz.

Today, Maine offers the mariner a whole parliament of boat yards for repairs or as bases for transient seafarers to leap frog up the coast. For you experienced salts who know what the "Charlie Noble" is, or for the new sailors, the data following should be very helpful.

Maine State Development Office photo

SALTWATER BOAT YARDS & MARINAS

Boat yard or Marina	Fuel G	Fuel D	Hauling Service Max. Length	Mast Stepping	Anchorage Overnight	Restaurants	Special Features
Arundel Shipyard Kennebunkport, 04046 (207) 967-5550			50'	Yes	Tie-ups	Many good choices	Wood Boat Restoration
Bar Harbor Boating Co. Hulls Cove, 04644 (207) 288-5797	x		40'	Yes	Yes	Acadian	
Bass Harbor Marina Bass Harbor, 04653 (207) 244-5066	x	x	60' 30 tons	Yes	Yes	Deck House	
Billings Diesel & Marine Stonington, 04681 (207) 367-2328	x	x	90' 4 railways	Yes	Yes	Fisherman's Friend— 1-mile	Build Wooden Boats
The Boathouse & Chandlery Shore Rd. Southwest Harbor, 04679 (207) 244-5561	x		25'		Yes	The Moorings	

Boat yard or Marina	Fuel G	Fuel D	Hauling Service Max. Length	Mast Stepping	Anchorage Overnight	Restaurants	Special Features
Dion Yacht Yard P. O. Box 486 Kittery, 03904 (207) 439-9582	Near By		72'	Yes	Yes		Rebuild — Repair — Over road Boat Transport
Eaton's Boat Yard Castine, 04421 (207) 326-8579	x	x	40'	Yes	Yes	Dennett's Castine Inn	
Goudy & Stevens East Boothbay, 04544	x		90'	Yes	Yes	Lobsterman's Wharf	
Handy Boat Service Falmouth F'side, 04105 (207) 781-5110	x		50'	Yes	Yes	Galley	
Harborside West Box 693 Camden, 04843 (207) 236-3264	x		25'	Yes Small	Yes	Available	
Harraseeket Marine So. Freeport, 04032 (207) 865-3181	x	x	50' 25 ton lift	Yes	Yes	Harraseeket Lunch & Lobster	Small Boat Rental

Henry Hinkley Co. Southwest Harbor, 04679 (207) 244-5531		x	Yes	Yes	Yes	The Mooring	
Knight Marina Rockland, 04841 (207) 594-4068	x	x	50' 18 tons	Yes	Yes	Black Pearl	
Lehtinen Boat Yard Tenants Harbor, 04860 (207) 372-6327			60'	Yes	Yes	Eastwind Hotel	
Longreach Co. 119 Commercial St. Bath, 04530 (207) 443-4771	x		Yes		Yes	J.R. Maxwell's	Walking distance to Maine Maritime Museum
Mt. Desert Yacht Yard Mt. Desert, 04660 (207) 276-5114			50' 25 tons	Yes	Yes	Kimble Terrace Popplestone	
Muscongus Marina Muscongus Road Medomak, 04551 (207) 529-5357	x	x	34'		Yes		

Boat yard or Marina	Fuel G	Fuel D	Hauling Service Max. Length	Mast Stepping	Anchorage Overnight	Restaurants	Special Features
New Meadows Marina 5541 Bath Road Brunswick, 04401 (207) 443-6277	x		40-50'	Yes	Yes	New Meadows Inn	Tops & Canvasses made to order
Pierce Marina P.O. Box 85 Boothbay Harbor, 04538 (207) 633-2922	x	x	Yes	Yes	Yes	Brown's Wharf	Beautiful sunsets
Robinhood Marina Robinhood Center, 04530 (207) 371-2525	x		50'		Yes	Osprey	
Rockport Marina, Inc., Box 203 Rockport, 04856 (207) 236-9651	x		43'	Yes	Yes	Sail Loft	Repairs — Rebuild Wooden Boats
Ring's Marine Service, So. Freeport, 04078 (207) 865-6143	x		60'	Yes			

Riverside Boat Co. Newcastle, 04553 (207) 563-3398		40' 12 tons	Yes	Yes Small	Cheechako Diner	
Rumery's Boatyard P.O. Box 6 Biddeford, 04005 (207) 282-0408	X	52' 24 tons	Yes			
Samples Shipyard P.O. Box 462 Boothbay Harbor, 04538 (207) 633-3171	X	150'	Yes	Yes	Many available	
Southwest Boat Corp. Box 117 Southwest Harbor, 04679 (207) 244-5525	X	100'	Yes	Yes	Beal's Lobster Pier	Showers & rest- rooms
Spring Point Marina Box 2277 So. Portland, 04106 (207) 767-3254	X	Yes	Yes	Yes	Quarterdeck	Very large marina
Spruce Head Marina P.O. Box 140 Spruce Head, 04859 (207) 594-7545		50'	Yes	Yes	Island Store —light lunch	Welding & Fabri- cation

Boat yard or Marina	Fuel G	D	Hauling Service Max. Length	Mast Stepping	Anchorage Overnight	Restaurants	Special Features
Wallace Marina RFD #2, Box 2075 Brunswick, 04011 (207) 729-1639	x	x	50' or 15 tons	Yes	Yes Limited		
Wayfarer Marine Corp. Sea St., Camden, 04843 (207) 236-4378	x	x	100'		Yes	Good Choices	Marine Store Laundromat
Winter Harbor Marina Winter Harbor, 04693 (207) 963-7449	x		40'	Yes	Yes	Chases & Fisherman's Inn	
Yarmouth Boat Yarmouth, 04096 (207) 846-4143	x		50' 20 tons	Yes	Yes	Anchor out	Connors Variety Store Small Rest.
York Harbor Marina York, 03909 (207) 363-3602	x	x	65'	Yes	Tie-ups	Dockside	

12 Freshwater Marinas

Marina	Lake	Services
Beaver Cove Marina Rodney Fulsom, Box 185, Greenville, ME 04441 Tel. (207) 695-3526	Moosehead Lake	Docking, 30 slips, repairs, storage, transport 23′
Cobbossee Marina Randy Gannett, Pond Road Manchester, ME 04351 Tel. (207) 724-3982	Cobbossee- contee Lake	Rentals — boat/ canoe, service, fuel, storage, launch ramp to 25′
Day's Marina Dave Harriman Box 276 Belgrade Lakes, ME 04918 Tel. (207) 495-2232	Belgrade Lakes	Moorings, storage, rent, gas, repairs, wood & fiberglass
Great Pond Marina Rt. 27 Belgrade Lakes, ME 04918 Tel. (207) 495-2213	Belgrade Lakes	Sales, service, rentals, ski boats, sail- boats, canoes, sailboards, storage to 23′
Mooselookmeguntic House Ed Kfoury Haines Marina Landing, Rangeley, ME 04970 Tel. (207) 864-3627	Rangeley Area	Storage, docking, gas, repair
Richard's Boat Yard Richard E. Richard- son R. #1, Box 436 White's Bridge Road, North Windham, ME 04062 Tel. (207) 892-4913	Sebago Lake	Docking, storage, service, repairs, boats transported

13 Marker Buoys

Remember: "Red on the right returning."

Red Nun

A red, tapered buoy marking the right side of a ship channel upon entering from seaward, or location of obstruction to be passed by keeping buoy on the right of the ship.

Lighted Buoy

Warns of underwater obstruction. The color of light indicates type of buoy at night.

Black Can

Marks the left side of the ship channel for ship approaching from seaward, or location of obstruction to be passed by keeping buoy on the left of ship.

Channel

Black and white vertically striped buoys mark middle of channel, should be passed close-to, on either side.

Obstruction

Alternating horizontal black and red striped buoy, marks either junction in ship channel or location of underwater obstruction to be passed on either side.

Day Beacon

Unlighted navigational aids are called Day Beacons, varying in design and construction, colored to distinguish them from their surroundings, and marked or numbered depending upon their purpose. Placed on land or reefs.

Spar

Long, tapered pole projecting above water, and appropriately painted or numbered to denote purpose.

Bell Buoy

Steel floats surmounted by skeleton towers in which a bell is attached. Sounded by motion of the water.

■ Fishing

14 Freshwater Rules

Nothing is so permanent as change! Maine's laws affecting fishing are no exception. I have listed below some definitions you should find helpful along with rules and regulations that do seem to be static.

1. **Fishing** is intended to include any attempt to take, catch, kill or destroy fish, successful or otherwise.
2. **Fly** (not the household type) is a single pointed hook to which feathers, hair, tinsel, etc. has been attached and (this is important) to which no weights (you nymph people need to note this) or spinners, etc. have been added.
3. **Fly fishing** means casting the fly (unweighted) in the usual manner of fly casting. Waters shown as "fly fishing only" do not allow you to troll a fly. It must be cast.
4. **Maine has a two line per person limit** during open water fishing. (Five lines during ice fishing although there is current pressure to reduce to 2 lines).
5. **Night fishing** is O.K. during open water.
6. **Baiting** is against the law. You cannot lug along some tasty morsels to be deposited in the water in an attempt to attract fish. This applies to open water and ice fishing. (O.K. for salt water, generally referred to as "chumming.")
7. **Selling fish** is illegal.

8. **Opening and closing dates** vary in some circumstances.
   Lakes and ponds open April 1–close Sept. 30.
   Rivers open April 1–close Sept. 15.
   Brooks and streams open April 1–close August 15.
9. **Minimum lengths of fish** have a tendency to vary, and
   certain waterways have special regulations that allow a
   decrease or increase in size. The following is generally
   true.

Fish Type	Lakes & Ponds	Brooks & Streams
Salmon	14	14
Lake Trout (Togue)	18	18
Brown Trout	12	6
Rainbow Trout	12	6
Brook Trout	6	6
Black Bass (small & large)	10	10
Other Species	No length restrictions	

10. **Symbols frequently used:**
    NLFAB   No live fish as bait
    FFO   Fly fishing only

Watch out for this one!

You cannot cut the head or tails from fish unless:
1. The remaining length meets the minimum length
   for that species.
2. You are preparing to cook **immediately.**

For accurate, up-to-date, and full coverage of *all* laws and
regulations, request:

Open Water Fishing Regulations
Maine Department of Inland
        Fisheries & Wildlife
284 State Street
Station #41
Augusta, ME 04333

15 Ice Fishing Rules

1. It is illegal to possess more than one day's limit during ice fishing season.
2. Where county lines divide a water, the more liberal county's rules apply.
3. The general daily bag limit for salmon, trout, and togue is 10 fish, of which not more than five can be taken from any or all lakes or ponds. The daily limit cannot include more than two salmon, two togue, three rainbow trout, or three brown trout.
4. In Androscoggin, Cumberland, Oxford, and York counties the daily limit on salmon, trout, and togue from any or all inland waters is five fish, not to include more than two salmon, two togue, three brown trout, or three rainbow trout. All five may be brook trout, except from lakes and ponds in Cumberland and York counties, where not more than three may be brook trout.
5. In Washington County the daily limit on salmon, trout, and togue is three fish in any combination.
6. In addition to these limits, it is illegal to catch more

than 7½ pounds of salmon, trout, or togue in any one day unless the last fish increases the combined weight to more than 7½ pounds.

7. The daily limit on black bass is five fish, maximum combined weight 7½ pounds, except the last fish caught may increase the combined weight to more than 7½ pounds.

8. Other limits are 10 pickerel, 8 whitefish, and two quarts of smelts. There are no bag limits on other species.

9. Minimum length limits for ice fishing on lakes and ponds are: salmon, 14 inches; togue, 18 inches; brown trout, 12 inches; rainbow trout, 12 inches; black bass, 10 inches; brook trout, 6 inches.

10. Minimum length limits for brooks, streams, and rivers are: salmon, 14 inches; togue, 18 inches; brown trout, 6 inches; rainbow trout, 12 inches; black bass, 10 inches; brook trout, 6 inches.

11. In Cumberland, Oxford, and York counties the minimum length limit on brook trout is 8 inches. The minimum length limit on brown trout and rainbow trout in Washington County streams and rivers is 8 inches.

12. Ice fishing is legal from the time ice forms in the winter through March 31. However, ice fishing for salmon, trout, and togue doesn't start until January 1.

CAUTION: Special laws apply to most Maine lakes and ponds for ice fishing. Check the latest law book before picking the water you want to fish. You may request ice fishing regulations from the same address as open water regulations. It is listed in the previous section.

16 Lake Depth Maps

Thomas Jefferson once said that those who don't read newspapers are better off than those who do because it was better to be uninformed than misinformed! If Jefferson had been a fisherman he would have required everyone to be able to read, only he'd have them reading depth maps.

Most major lakes in Maine have been surveyed as to depth. This is an invaluable source of data for the serious fisherman. Depths are clearly marked over all locations on the lake. Reefs, shoals, deep holes are easy to find. These are excellent aids to catching fish in Maine. Smelts are the major forage for game fish, and these maps will help you locate the most promising areas.

Note: An index to all Maine lakes which have been surveyed as to depth may be ordered directly from the Department of Inland Fisheries and Wildlife, 284 State Street, Station #41, Augusta, ME 04333.

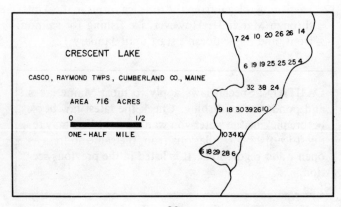

DATE 1983	WATERS STOCKED	TOWN	SPECIES	AMOUNT	INCH
MAY 2	PEABODY POND	SEBAGO	L.L. SALMON	400	8 - 10
MAY 2	PANTHER POND	RAYMOND	" "	550	8 - 10
MAY 27	LONG LAKE	HARRISON	" "	1045	8 - 10
MAY 2	PLEASANT LAKE	CASCO	" "	500	8 - 10
MAY 2	THOMPSON LAKE	OTISFIELD	" "	1500	8 - 10
JUN 1	SEBAGO LAKE	SEBAGO	" "	1000	8 - 10
MAY 25	PLEASANT POND	CASCO	" "	6	16 - 18
APR 28	LITTLE RIVER	GORHAM	BROWN TROUT	1000	6 - 8
APR 28	PRESUMPSCOT RIVER	WESTBROOK	" "	1500	6 - 8
APR 29	PISCATAQUA RIVER	FALMOUTH	" "	500	6 - 8
APR 29	ROYAL RIVER	NEW GLOUCESTER	" "	1000	6 - 8
MAY 4	ROYAL RIVER	YARMOUTH	" "	3000	6 - 8
MAY 4	PLEASANT RIVER	WINDHAM	" "	1000	6 - 8
OCT 6	WATCHIC LAKE	STANDISH	" "	450	10 - 12
OCT 6	HIGHLAND LAKE	WINDHAM	" "	1200	10 - 12
OCT 7	WOODS POND	BRIDGTON	" "	600	10 - 12
OCT 7	HIGHLAND LAKE	BRIDGTON	" "	800	10 - 12
OCT 13	CRYSTAL POND	GRAY	" "	500	10 - 12
OCT 13	SABBATHDAY LAKE	NEW GLOUCESTER	" "	700	10 - 12
OCT 17	RAYMOND POND	RAYMOND	" "	850	10 - 12
NOV 29	HIGHLAND LAKE	WINDHAM	" "	50	14 - 16
APR 14	CRYSTAL LAKE	HARRISON	LAKE TROUT	600	6 - 8
APR 11	PANTHER POND	RAYMOND	" "	3500	6 - 8
APR 15	LONG LAKE	HARRISON	" "	7200	6 - 8
APR 11	PEABODY POND	NAPLES	" "	1500	6 - 8
APR 11	TRICKY POND	NAPLES	" "	1500	6 - 8
APR 12	MOOSE POND	BRIDGTON	" "	2400	6 - 8
APR 12	PLEASANT POND	CASCO	" "	3500	6 - 8
APR 25	PINELAND POND	POWNAL	BROOK TROUT	200	8 - 10
APR 19	PEABODY POND	SEBAGO	" "	1000	8 - 10
APR 25	HINCKLEY POND	SOUTH PORTLAND	" "	200	8 - 10

17 Stocking Reports

A large majority of Maine's cold, clear lakes are stocked annually with salmon, trout, togue (lake trout), and browns.

A list of stockings may be obtained from the Department of Inland Fisheries and Wildlife, 284 State Street, Station #41, Augusta, ME 04333. The current price is $1.00. By back ordering the previous three years you can see where some trophy size fish might be taken.

A sample of a stocking report is shown: **Cumberland County.**

18 Fish Hatcheries

Bring the whole family for an educational experience. Maine relies heavily upon its hatchery system to support its excellent fishing. **Note:** Hatchery stations actually hatch the eggs. Rearing stations take over and rear the fingerlings to the stage where they are ready for stocking in lakes and streams.

Cobb State Fish Hatchery Enfield (Map Key F-6) Open to public. Landlocked salmon and brook trout are raised here for future stocking. Open daily 8:00–4:00.

Craig Brook National Fish Hatchery (Federal Program) Orland (Map Key E-6) Opened in 1871, it now cultures Atlantic Salmon. Visitors can use the nature trail, see live fish in display pools. Picnic area. Open all year 8:00–8:00.

Dry Mills State Fish Hatchery Dry Mills (Map Key C-2) Opened to public in 1934. Currently raising brook trout, lake trout (togue), and brown trout. Open daily May 1 to Nov. 1. *Interesting note:* State game farm is adjacent to the hatchery. Visitors can see deer, bear, moose, small animals, and birds.

Ela Fish Rearing Station Emden (Map Key F-3) Opened 1956 to rear brook trout and salmon. Open all year 8:00–4:00.

Governor Hill State Fish Hatchery Augusta (Map Key D-3,4) Began 1923, originally private, now belongs to State. Raises lake trout (togue), splake (a cross between togue and brook trout), and brook trout. Open to public 8:00–4:00 year round.

Grand Lake Stream Fish Hatchery (Federal program) Grand Lake Stream (Map Key F-8) Founded 1875. New site is modern, with land locked salmon its major fish. First fish hatchery in nation to have a screen to filter out minute particles from incoming water which is then subjected to ultraviolet light—gives "pure" water. Open to public. Call ahead for this one. Tel. (207) 796–5580. Eggs from here go all over the world!

Green Lake National Fish Hatchery Ellsworth (Map Key E-7) Opened 1974 to production of Atlantic Salmon for restoration of salmon in Maine. Juvenile Atlantic Salmon can be seen in various growth stages. Guided tours for groups by appointment. Open all year 7:30–4:00.

New Gloucester State Fish Hatchery New Gloucester (Map Key C-2) Opened in 1934. Currently raising brown trout for sport fishing. Visitors can see browns in all stages of growth. Open every day 8 hours.

Palermo State Rearing Station Palermo (Map Key D-4) Currently brown trout are reared here from eggs. Often rear other species of fish. Open to public 8:00–4:00 year round.

Wade State Fish Hatchery Casco (Map Key C-2) Opened in 1954 to raise landlocked salmon. Visitors can see 2 to 3 lb. show fish, albino salmon 6″ to 8″ and production salmon. Open year round 8:00–4:00.

19 Saltwater Directory

MAINE SALT WATER FISHING DIRECTORY

X = Year-round
S = Seasonal

	Cod	Haddock	Cusk	Hake S & B	Pollock	Flounder	Halibut	Mackerel	Striper	Smelt	Tuna	Salmon	Shad	Cunner	Hbr. Pollock
Eliot								S	S						
Kittery	X	X	X	X	X	X	S	S	S	X	S			X	X
Piscataqua River					S			S		X				X	X
Spruce Creek					S			S	S					X	X
Great Bay					X			S	X					X	X
York	X	X	X	X	X	X	S	S	S	X	S			X	X
Brave Boat Harbor					X			S	X					X	X
York River					X			S	S	X					X
Cape Neddick River					X			S						X	X
Wells	X	X	X	X	X	X	S	S	S			S		X	X
Ogunquit River								S					X		
Webhannet River								S							X
Little River								S							X

X = Year-round
S = Seasonal

	Cod	Haddock	Cusk	Hake S & B	Pollock	Flounder	Halibut	Mackerel	Striper	Smelt	Tuna	Salmon	Shad	Cunner	Hbr. Pollock
Kennebunk															
Mousam River									S					X	X
Kennebunk River									S				S	X	X
Kennebunkport	X	X	X	X	X	X	S	S	S	S	X	S	S	X	X
Turbats Creek						S		S						X	X
Patty Creek						S		S						X	X
Porpoise Creek						S		S						X	X
Batson River						S		S						X	X
Little River						S		S						X	X
Biddeford	X	X	X	X	X	X	S	S	S	S	X	S		X	X
Saco River								S	X					S	S
Saco	X	X	X	X	X	X		S	X	S				X	X
Goosefare Brook						S		S							
Old Orchard Beach and Ocean Park															S
Pine Point	X	X	X	X	X	X	S	S	S	S	S	S		X	X
Scarboro River						S		S	S						S
Dunston River						S		S							
Nonesuch River						S		S				S			
Scarborough						S		S							
Spurwink River						S		S							
Portland	X	X	X	X	X	X	S	S			X	S		X	X
Presumpscot River															
South Portland	X	X	X	X	X	X	S	S			X	S		X	X
Cape Elizabeth	X	X	X	X	X	X	S	S	S			S		X	X
Cumberland	S	S	S	S	S	S	S	S	S	S	S	S			S
Falmouth	S	S	S	S	S	S	S	S	S	S	S	S			S
Yarmouth	S	S	S	S	S	S	S	S	S	S	S			S	S
Royal River						S		S	S	S					S
Cousins River						S		S	S	S					S
Freeport	S	S	S	S	S	S	S	S	S	S	S	S		S	S
Harraseeket River								S	S	S					X
Harpswell	X	X	X	S	X	X	X	S	S	S	X	S			X
Bailey & Orrs Island	X	X	X	S	X	X	X	S	S	S	X	S		X	X
Brunswick								S	S						

X = Year-round
S = Seasonal

	Cod	Haddock	Cusk	Hake S & B	Pollock	Flounder	Halibut	Mackerel	Striper	Smelt	Tuna	Salmon	Shad	Cunner	Hbr. Pollock
Middle Bay								S	S	S					X
Harpswell Sound								S	S	S					X
Quahog Bay								S	S						X
New Meadows River								S	S	S					X
West Bath					S			S	S	X					S
Phippsburg	X	X	X	S	X	X	S	S	S	S	S	S	S	X	X
Bath								S	S	S					
Kennebec River (lower)								S	S	S					X
Kennebec River (upper)									S	S					
Arrowsic						X		S	S	S					X
Sasanoa River						X		S	S	S					X
Georgetown	X	X	X	S	X	X	X	S	S	X	S	S	S	X	X
Back River						X		S	S	S					
Woolwich						X		S	S	S					X
Montsweag Bay						X			S	S					X
Robinhood Cove						X			S	S					X
Knubble Bay						X			S	S					X
Westport	X	X	X	S	X	X		S	S	X	S	S	S	X	X
Wiscasset	X	X	X	S	X	X		S	S	X	S	S	S	X	X
Sheepscot River (lower)	X	X	X	S	X	X		S	S	X	S	S	S	X	X
Sheepscot River (upper)									S	X		S	S		
Edgecomb	X	X	X	S	X	X		S	S	X	S	S	S	X	X
Marsh River*									S	X					X
Boothbay Harbor	X	X	X	X	X	X	S	S	S	X	S			X	X
Southport	X	X	X	X	X	X	S	S	S	X	S			X	X
Boothbay	X	X	X	X	X	X	S	S	S	X	S			X	X
Damariscotta River						X		S	S	X				X	X
Newcastle						X		S	S	X				X	X
Damariscotta	S	S	S	S	S	S	S	S	S	X	S			S	S
Damariscotta Bay						X		S	X						X
South Bristol	X	X	X	X	X	X	X	S	S	X	S			X	X
Monhegan	X	X	X	X	X	X	S	S				S		X	X

*Occasional

MAINE SALT WATER FISHING DIRECTORY

X = Year-round
S = Seasonal

	Cod	Haddock	Cusk	Hake S & B	Pollock	Flounder	Halibut	Mackerel	Striper	Smelt	Tuna	Salmon	Shad	Cunner	Hbr. Pollock
Bristol	X	X	X	X	X	X	X	S	S	X	S			X	X
Pemaquid River						X		S	S	X				X	X
Bremen						X		S	S	X					X
Muscongus Bay						X		S	S	X					X
Medomak River						X		S	S	X					X
Waldoboro						X		S	S						
Friendship	S			S	S	S	S	S	S	S					S
Cushing			S			S	S	S	S						X
Warren								S	S						
St. George River								S	S						
St. George															
South Thomaston								S	S						
Weskeag River								S	S						
Thomaston	S	S	S	S	S	S	S	S	S	S				S	S
St. George River								S	S	S				S	S
Penobscot Bay	X	X	X	X	X	X	S	S	S	X				X	X
Tenants Harbor	X	X		X	X	S	S	S	S	S				X	
Port Clyde	X	X		X	X	S	S	S	S	S				X	
Owls Head	X	X		X	X	S	S	S	S	S				X	
Rockland	X	X	X	X	X	X	S	S	S	X				X	X
Rockport	X	X	X	X	X	X	S	S	S	X				X	X
Camden	X	X	X	X	X	X	S	S	S	X				X	X
Lincolnville	X	X	X	X	X	X	S	S	S	X				X	X
Ducktrap River									S			S			
Northport	S					S		S	S	X					S
Belfast	S					S		S	S	X					S
Searsport	S					S		S	S	X					S
Stockton Springs	S					S		S	S	X					S
Frankfort									S	X					
Penobscot									S	X		S			
Bucksport	S					S		S	S	X					S
Verona	S					S		S	S	X					S
Penobscot River						S		S	S	X					S
Castine	X	X	X	X	X	X	S	S	S	X				X	X

94

X = Year-round
S = Seasonal

	Cod	Haddock	Cusk	Hake S & B	Pollock	Flounder	Halibut	Mackerel	Striper	Smelt	Tuna	Salmon	Shad	Cunner	Hbr. Pollock
Bagaduce River					S		S	S	X					X	X
Penobscot Bay Island															
Islesboro	X	X		X	X	S	S	S	S	S				X	X
North Haven	X	X		X	X	S	S	S		S				X	X
Vinalhaven	X	X		X	X	S	S	S		S				X	X
Isle au Haut	X	X		X	X	S	S	S		S				X	X
Matinicus	X	X		X	X	S	S	S		S				X	X
Brooksville															
Sedgwick															
Eggemoggin Reach															
Deer Isle	X	X			X	X	S	S		X					X
Stonington	X	X		X	X	X	S	S		X					X
Brooklin	S	S				X		S		X					S
Blue Hill	S	S				X		S		X					S
Salt Pond						X		S		X					S
Blue Hill Bay						X		S		X					S
Surry						X		S	S	S				X	X
Patten Bay						X		S	S	S				X	X
Ellsworth						X			S	S				X	X
Union River						X			S	S				X	X
Trenton						X		S	S	X					X
Eastern Bay						X		S	S	X					X
Western Bay						X		S	S	X					X
Mt. Desert Island	X	X	X	X	X	X	S	S		X				X	X
Bar Harbor	X	X	X	X	X	X	S	S		X				X	X
Mt. Desert	X	X	X	X	X	X	S			X				X	X
Somes Sound						X		S		S				X	X
Tremont	X	X	X	X	X	X	S	S			S			X	X
Southwest Harbor	X	X	X	X	X	X	S	S			S			X	X
Cranberry Island	X	X	X	X	X	X	S	S			S				X
Swan Island	X	X	X	X	X	X	S	S			S				X
Frenchboro	X	X	X	X	X	X	S	S			S				X
Lamoine	S	S		S	S	X		S		X				X	X
Hancock															
Skillings River															

MAINE SALT WATER FISHING DIRECTORY

X = Year-round
S = Seasonal

	Cod	Haddock	Cusk	Hake S & B	Pollock	Flounder	Halibut	Mackerel	Striper	Smelt	Tuna	Salmon	Shad	Cunner	Hbr. Pollock
Taunton River & Bay								S	S	X					X
Franklin									S	X					X
Sullivan									S	X					X
Sorrento	X	X	X	X	X	X		S		S					X
Flanders Bay								S		S					X
Gouldsboro	X	X	X	X	X	X		S							X
Gouldsboro Bay					S					S					S
Winter Harbor	X	X	X	X	X	X		S		S					X
Steuben	X	X	X	X	X	X		S		S					X
Dyer Bay					S										S
Narraguagus River									S	S		S	S		S
Milbridge	S	S	S	S	S	S			S	S		S	S		S
Flat Bay					S										
Cherryfield									S			S			
Columbia									S			S	S		
Harrington	X	X	X	X	X	S									
Harrington River	X	X	X	X	X	S			S				S		S
Addison	X	X	X	X	X										
Indian River															
Columbia Falls									S	S	S				
Pleasant River									S		S				
Jonesboro															
Chandler River															
Jonesport & Beals Island	X	X	X	X	X	X	S	S						S	S
Roque Bluffs						S		S						S	X
Little Kennebec River						S		S		S			S		
Machiasport	X	X	X	X	X	X	S	S	S	S		S	S	S	X
Machias									S	S		S			
Machias River									S	S		S			
East Machias									S	S		S			
East Machias River									S	S		S			
Holmes Bay										S					
Machias Bay	X	X	X	X	X	X								X	X
Whiting															
Cutler	X	X	X	X	X	X			S					X	X

96

X = Year-round
S = Seasonal

	Cod	Haddock	Cusk	Hake S & B	Pollock	Flounder	Halibut	Mackerel	Striper	Smelt	Tuna	Salmon	Shad	Cunner	Hbr. Pollock
Little Machias Bay	X	X		X	X	X								X	X
Trescott	X	X		X	X	X	S	S		S				X	X
Lubec	X	X		X	X	X	S	S		X				X	X
Edmunds					S					X					
Dennysville					S			S		X		S	S		
Dennys River					S			S		X		S	S		
Whiting Bay					S			S		X		S	S		
Pembroke					S					X					
Pennamaquan								S			S				X
Perry	X	X		X	X	X	X	S	S					X	X
Eastport	X	X		X	X	X	X			S				X	X
Cobscook Bay	X	X		X	X	X	X							X	X
Robbinston	X	X		X	X	X	X	S	S					X	X
Calais								S	S			S	S		
St. Croix River								S	S			S	S		

20 Saltwater Rules

Shellfish In Maine, towns control regulations on clamming, usually through a local clam warden. Some towns permit recreational digging as long as the amount does not exceed a half bushel per day. Your best action would be to check with the town office prior to digging!

There is no limit on the number of crabs you may keep but lobsters are carefully regulated. You must have a commercial license to "fish" lobsters.

Marine worms   125 worms may be dug for personal use per day.

Striped Bass   4 stripers may be kept per day, minimum length 16 inches.

Salmon   1 Atlantic Salmon is the limit per day, with a minimum length of 14 inches (artificial lures only). Two coho salmon may be taken per day with minimum length of 14 inches.

Marine Resources Warden Headquarters

Division I   South Portland Regional Office
c/o SMVTI
Fort Rd.
South Portland, ME 04106
Tel. (207) 799–7303 (ext. 214) or 799–3380

Division II   Rockland Regional Office
Box 931
Rockland, ME 04841
Tel. (207) 594–7774

Division III   Ellsworth Regional Office
P.O. Box 674
Ellsworth, ME 04605
Tel. (207) 667–3127

---

21 Atlantic Salmon

Atlantic Salmon fishing for many anglers is *the only* fish worth gearing up for. Maine's Penobscot River provides the best rod and reel catches in the U.S. While there are ups and downs, the Penobscot has proved a consistent producer . . . but not the only one.

Listed below are river locations, flies that are productive, available lodging, plus directions to fishing locations.

River Locations	Productive Flies	Lodging
Dennys River Dennysville (Map Key E-10)	Rusty Rat, Cosseboom	Lincoln House Country Inn Dennysville (207) 726-3953
East Machias River Machias (Map Key E-9)	Rusty Rat, Green Butt, Cosseboom, Yellow Bomber	Mainland Motel Machias (207) 255-3334
Machias River Machias (Map Key E-9)	Butterfly, Cosseboom	Bluebird Motel Machias (207) 255-3332
Narraguagus River Cherryfield (Map Key E-8)	Green Butt, Thunder & Lightning, Rusty Rat, Bomber	Howard's Motel Millbridge (207) 546-7721
Penobscot River Bangor & Veazie (Map Key E-6)	Mickey Finn, Green Butt, Red Butt, Cosseboom	Ebb Tide Motel Brewer (207) 989-3370
Penobscot River Brewer & Eddington (Map Key E-6)	Coburn Special, Thunder & Lightning, Ringer	Holiday Inn Bangor Main St. (207) 947-8651 Adlin Road (207) 947-0101)

DIRECTIONS TO FISHING SITES

Dennys River   Rt. 1 to Dennysville, left on Rt. 86. Pools from bridge downstream to village.

East Machias River   Rt. 1 to East Machias Village, cross bridge to Rt. 191, pools from old power dam north to green bridge north of village.

Machias River   Rt. 1 to Machias. Pools: tidal water below falls in Machias Village; west on Rt. 1A to Whitneyville, north of Whitneyville at Great Falls.

Narraguagus River   Rt. 1 north to Cherryfield, left on Rt. 193 north. Pools on east and west shores of river from school in village (Academy) north to ice dam above Cable Pool.

Penobscot River—West Shore (Bangor—Veazie)   I-95 to Bangor, exit 46 to Rt. 2 north to Veazie, right at blinker. Pools from Veazie Dam (power station) south along shore.

Penobscot River—East Shore (Brewer to Eddington)   I-95 to Bangor, I-395 to Rt. 9/178 north, cross bridge to Brewer, left (north) on Rt. 9/178. Pools from Brewer (Bangor Salmon Club) north to North Eddington on Rt. 178.

SHOPS THAT SPECIALIZE IN ATLANTIC SALMON FLIES

Bob Leeman's Trout Shop   Brewer, ME 04412, Tel. (207) 989-5538

Charles Shoppe   West Franklin, ME 04634, Tel. (207) 565-3350

Eddie's Flies   Bangor, ME 04401, Tel. (207) 945-5587

Kittery Trading Post   Kittery, ME 03904, Tel. (207) 439-2700

L. L. Bean's   Freeport, ME 04032, Tel. 1-800-221-4221

LAND

(cont'd)

■ Hiking Trails

The hikes shown below have been divided into beginner, intermediate, and advanced groups. There are no special techniques needed for these trips nor any special equipment. These are not technical mountains requiring ropes, rappelling, etc. Bring a backpack and a healthy body.

Trails are periodically changed to prevent erosion. Before going on one of the hikes described contact the forest ranger in the district, the Appalachian Mountain Club, 5 Joy Street, Boston, MA or The Maine A.T. Club, Inc., Box 283, Augusta, ME 04330.

Two books that will be extremely helpful are:

Fifty Hikes in Maine by John Gibson, New Hampshire Publishing Company, Somersworth, N.H.

Fifty More Hikes in Maine by Cloe Catlett, New Hampshire Publishing Company, Somersworth, N.H.

22 Beginner Hikes

1. Gulf Hagas
2. Streaked Mountain
3. Mount Kineo
4. Mount Megunticook
5. Bald Mountain
6. Pleasant Mountain
7. Mount Blue

1. GULF HAGAS
Round trip 10 miles, vertical rise 600 feet, hiking time 7 hours (Map Key G-5)

The Gulf is really a canyon cut in rock eroded by the West Branch of the Pleasant River. As the key builder of the Gulf the river worries its way 2.5 miles through the gorge, dropping 500′ in this short span. The results are spectacular falls and sheer canyon walls, most all of which are visible from the trail that parallels the lip.

Starting Point   Rt. 11 to Brownville Junction, 4 miles north turn left (west) at the sign reading Katahdin Iron Works, drive 6.5 miles to the Works. Register here and receive a Diamond Company map (which is more useful here than your USGS map). Drive over the bridge, take right fork—stay on widest road offered. At 3.4 miles bear left and recross the Pleasant River. The Appalachian Trail (AT) crosses this road at the 7 mile mark. Park off road by small bridge.

The Climb   Follow white blazes to the right (north). At .7 miles cross the West Branch to the Hermitage (this is a grove of 130 year old white pine). At one mile intersect the Old Pleasant River Road, turn left (west), note sign—1.1 miles to Screw Auger Falls. Plan to take a short .2 mile side trip to Screw Auger, a pretty 26′ waterfall, then retrace to blue blazed trail. Note the split in the loop trail. It is better to hike all the way in on the northerly trail then return along the lip of the gorge on the southern route. On your Diamond map, note trails to Hammond Street Pitch (90′ cliff), Indian Head, Lower and Upper Jaws, Buttermilk Falls, Stair Falls and Billings Falls.

2. STREAKED MOUNTAIN
1 ½ miles round trip, vertical rise 750 feet, hiking time one hour   (Map Key D-2)

Streaked Mt. is one of the handy affairs lending itself to the busy schedule and providing a nice day outing. Good views of the Presidentials, Evans Notch, and the Rumford-Weld area. Streaked is named for strips of open ledge on its SW exposure.

Starting Point   Turn SE onto a tar road leading from Rt. 117 (located 5 miles east of South Paris and 5 miles SW of Buckfield. Travel ⅔ mile to where a culvert crosses and power lines are located. Park on east side of road.

The Climb   Climb east-north-east over old jeep road running under the power lines, turn to the right still on jeep trail, then past junction of three lumber roads, then enter the ledges. Climb on the center of the ledge, then left of center near the top. The second band of ledges should be carried to the left. Reach the tower at the summit for excellent views.

3. KINEO MOUNTAIN
4 miles round trip, vertical rise 800 feet, hiking time 2½ hours   (Map Key G-4)

An 800′ granite bubble rises abruptly out of Moosehead, Maine's largest lake. Classic views of the lake and its surrounding mountains are available from the old fire tower atop the mountain. Indians traveled to this area to obtain Kineo Flint, used for arrows, spears, and knives.

Starting Point   Arrive in Greenville from the south, turn left following Rt. 6-15 for 20 miles to Rockwood. There used to be a public boat launch in town but this is no longer available. Several options exist. 1. Mr. Vance Lincoln runs a shuttle service to Kineo from May 1 to Oct. 1 with a fee in 1984 of $20 for two people, $5 each additional. Write to him at Rockwood, ME 04478. 2. Along the river, locate the Moose River Country Store. They have a boat ramp and charge a small fee to launch. Land at the dock at Kineo

Cove near the Kineo Hotel. The sheer face of the mountain can be seen here and is truly an impressive sight.

The Hike   From Kineo dock walk the dirt road along the edge of the old golf course, bear left at all forks. The path to the top is along water's edge. Huge cliffs of Kineo flint can be seen here. Approximately .6 mile from the dock the Indian Trail leaves to the right, uphill (look for worn trail—no sign). At .9 mile watch for unmarked trail to the left. The Bridle Trail, as this is called, will be used for your return route. Beyond the Bridle Trail continue upwards to a fork in the trail, bear left to the 1806′ summit and the abandoned fire tower. Views from here are outstanding.

Leave the fire tower and return on the arrival route for .3 mile. Watch for the Bridle Trail which leads down the mountain to the forest ranger's cabin on the lake shore. Follow the shore trail back to the hotel and the starting point.

4. MEGUNTICOOK MOUNTAIN
3½ miles round trip, vertical rise 1,150 feet, hiking time 2¼ hours   (Map Key D-5)

This is a real family hike with a postcard perfect view of Camden Harbor nestled at the foot of the mountain. The hike gives a good stretch to the legs but is not exhausting.

Starting Point   Arrive Camden via Rt. 1, drive north for approximately .2 mile to Camden State Park, turn left into the Park and leave your car in a convenient place. Locate the warden's shelter. The trail to Megunticook is NW of the shelter.

The Hike The trail rises gradually. There are no abrupt rises. At about .3 mile the trail swings to the right, soon after you can see Mt. Battie. The trail is steeper here as you approach the junction of Ocean Lookout and Tableland trails. Continue uphill beyond this junction to the summit.

The return trip can be a simple retracing, or take the Tableland trail to the col between Mt. Battie and Megunticook—good views here. 1¼ miles from Ocean Lookout find the Mt. Battie Road, descend along the road to the starting point.

5. BALD MOUNTAIN
3 miles round trip, vertical rise 1,400 feet, hiking time 2 hours   (Map Key E-2)

Excellent overlooks of Lake Webb (site of Mt. Blue State Park) can be obtained from Bald Mt. There are many "Bald" mountains in Maine. This one is between Weld and Wilton.

Starting Point The trail is on the right approximately 4 miles southeast of Weld on Rt. 156, or on the left 8 miles from Wilton. A sign marks the trail but the actual path may be obscured at the beginning. Once on the trail it becomes clear and rises through mixed hardwoods with some blazes. Keep a close watch for the trail on the lower section.

Shortly, you arrive above the timber line. Cairns mark the route to the summit. Jackson, Tumbledown, and Blueberry Mountains frame the north sky, with Mt. Blue due north.

6. PLEASANT MOUNTAIN
3½ miles round trip, vertical rise 1,500 feet, hiking time 3 hours   (Map Key C-1)

Singular in size for the area, Pleasant Mt. rises like a guardian over Moose Pond and houses the famous Pleasant Mt. ski area.

Starting Point Drive west 4 miles on Rt. 302 from Bridgton toward Fryeburg. Turn left on the road to the ski area (first left after Moose Pond). At .3 mile from Rt. 302 look for a pine tree with a red M painted on it. Park here but be sure to get your car completely off road. Moose Trail, sometimes referred to as the Ledges Trail, is marked by red blazes and begins ascending on a fire road. This gives way to a trail, then a fork. Bear left, cross two brooks. Here the climb is steeper as you approach the ledges (good place to rest and take in the view). You will pass through two more open ledges on the way to the summit.

The Presidentials in New Hampshire unfold from north to south together with fine vistas of Pleasant Pond, Lovewell Pond, and Fryeburg.

7. MOUNT BLUE
3¼ miles round trip, vertical rise 1,800 feet, hiking time 2½ hours   (Map Key E-2)

The perfect cone shape is the trademark of Mt. Blue, and the trail to the summit is a friendly host to hikers of all abilities.

Starting Point Turn off Rt. 142 in the town of Weld onto Maxwell Road, bear right all the way on main road to a grassy parking area about 6 miles from Weld.

The Hike Leave the parking area up a fire road heading NE. The climb here is "brisk" but not difficult. At ¾ miles you should be able to hear a brook on the left, a good water stop. At 1 mile find the abandoned warden's cabin, again on left, and soon after you will stride over the lower ridge. The vertical climb flattens somewhat, then stiffens up as you approach the summit. The top provides an excellent vantage point. On a clear day the 360° view is superb. Check it out.

---

23 Intermediate Hikes

---

1. Elephant Mountain
2. North Traveler
3. Cadillac Mountain
4. Tumbledown

5. Carlo-Goose Eye Loop
6. The Owl
7. Baldpate Mountain

1. ELEPHANT MOUNTAIN
11⅓ miles round trip, vertical rise 800 feet, hiking time six hours   (Map Key F-1)

Many hikers claim the lean-to shelter and its adjacent pond are the best location on the Appalachian Trail. Whatever your choice you will enjoy your climb on Elephant Mt.

Starting Point Leave Rt. 17 11.8 miles south of Oquossoc (due west of Rangeley). Start up the Bemis Trail (point where Appalachian Trail crosses).

The Hike The trail leads over an old road through a swamp barren, over a brook, into stands of spruce. The abandoned Maine Central R.R. right of way is reached at about 1.2 miles. Cross the railroad bed, then right onto a gravel road following this west & northwest, then left on a steep road southwest. Bemis Stream will come to the trail and cross to north at about 2¼ miles, cross a brook at 3½ miles, then follow a short piece of gravel road and re-enter thick woods heading west southwest. The gravel road continues to the right, do not follow this road. Cross another brook, then around a boulder marked "4 miles." At 5 miles, break over a low ridge where Elephant Mt. can be seen. Reach the lean-to at about 5½ miles. This lean-to is in poor repair but its location next to a small, boulder-strewn pond makes it very popular with hikers. As such be self-sufficient. This lean-to may be full, especially on weekends.

2. NORTH TRAVELER
5 miles round trip, vertical rise 1,175 feet, hiking time 3½ hours   (Map Key H-6)

A giant swimming in Grand Lake Matagamon might sit on the Travelers as he dried his feet! This northerly set of mountains in the Baxter chain has broad, smooth sides and peaks.

Starting Point   I-95 to Sherman Station, Rt. 11 to Patten, Rt. 159 to Shin Pond and Matagamon Wilderness Campground (excellent place to establish base camp). From the campground enter Baxter State Park and proceed to "the crossing." This is 33 miles west of Patten. Drive south to South Branch Campground, 1¾ miles from "the crossing." Camping is available here also. Write Baxter State Park Authority, 64 Balsam Drive, Millinocket, ME 04462 for information on campsite reservations.

Head up the Pogy Notch trail for ¼ mile, then left onto North Travelers trail. The hiking is quite gentle here, then

110

the rise increases to an uphill lift at the ledges and the peak. Outstanding views of the East Branch of the Penobscot and surrounding mountains (Bill Fish, Barrell Ridge, Traveler) are available from this summit.

3. CADILLAC MOUNTAIN
7 miles round trip, vertical rise 1,230 feet, hiking time 5 hours   (Map Key D-7)

A postcard mountain, that's Cadillac. The highest point on Mt. Desert Island, the overlooks are truly fantastic. Frenchmen's Bay, The Porcupine Islands, and Schoodic Peninsula make a beautiful Maine vista.

Starting Point   Someone once said, "No matter where you go, there you are." Well in this case where you are to start your hike is at *the top* of the mountain. Makes sense, you can drive there!

Arrive on the island via Rt. 198/102, turn left in Summerville on 198/3, bear left onto Rt. 233, turn right after Eagle Lake onto the Jordan Pond road, take second left to Cadillac Mt. Park at the top.

The Hike   Choose a clear day, the view from the top deserves this. Then enter the South Ridge Trail leading from the parking lot. Lots of ledges in the first mile with outcrops that give the hiker excellent scenery to photograph. At 1¼ miles you will cross a level area known as the "feather bed." Continue straight ahead to the loop to "Eagle Crag," a large rock outcrop giving good views east and southeast. Below the crag you enter woods to Rt. 3. Black Woods campground is directly across Rt. 3, and a short hike to the water is worth the effort. Retrace the same route to return to the top.

4. TUMBLEDOWN
4¹/₂ miles round trip (including loop), vertical rise 1,400 feet, hiking time 3¹/₂ hours   (Map Key E-2)

It seems all hikers have heard of "the Chimney" which probably accounts for Tumbledown's fame. There is a breadth of hiking experiences all nestled into the Byron Notch area.

Starting Point   Let's see how we do! In Weld Corner turn west off Rt. 142 onto the Byron Road, bear right at the fork, drive past the trail to Little Jackson Mt. and Parker Ridge. Approximately 3 miles beyond the Parker Ridge Trail look for the Chimney Trail. There are markers showing the beginning point. Park to the left.

The Hike   Some ideas to keep in mind. The approach to the Chimney is over a pile of boulders which can be hazardous in wet weather. If you are inexperienced it might be better to go up to *and* down from the summit via the Loop Trail.

Enter the trail off the Byron Road into the woods and a relatively level walk over a ridge and through a boggy spot. The trail stiffens up as you find the balanced rock at ½ mile and the huge boulder at 1 mile. The climb is now definitely uphill! In another ¼ mile locate the cairn where the trail splits, the Chimney left, the Loop right. Turn left onto Chimney (sign may be gone). There are lots of boulders! As you reach rock overhangs, beware of loose soil and sliding shale.

Climb up the gully to the base of the Chimney. The top is negotiated by using an iron ladder. The best views are not from the Chimney top, but the west summit.

The mountain offers an open ridge between the east and west summits which makes hiking here enjoyable. From the east peak watch for the Loop Trail which you follow back to the car.

5. CARLO-GOOSE EYE LOOP
7 1/4 miles round trip, vertical rise, 2,200 feet, hiking time 5 hours   (Map Key E-1)

This hike is included because it provides excellent overlooks of the Mahoosuc Mt. range, often referred to as the most difficult part of the Appalachian Trail. The area is wild, rugged and isolated.

Starting Point   For this climb drive to Berlin, New Hampshire, cross the bridge at Berlin Mills, turn left on Hutchins Street. Follow this route through pulp yards to a road known locally as the Success Pond Road (probably not marked). Turn right onto this road. Approximately 8½ miles in on this road watch for the Carlo Col trail on the right.

The Hike   The Carlo Col and Goose Eye trails overlay each other at the beginning. At the Brown Company sign, turn right onto the Carlo Col, proceed up a steep embankment and bear left onto an old logging road. Approximately ¾ mile the Col between Mt. Carlo and Mt. Success is visible. Keep to the left as you cross a brook. This climb steepens up, then runs right toward the Col. The trail narrows at 1¾ miles. At 2 miles start the steep ascent to the Col. Just below the Col is the Carlo Col shelter. The Mahoosuc trail is reached at 2⅔ miles. Here the trail to Carlo and Goose Eye turns left up a steep grade ½ mile to Carlo summit.

Travel northeast to Goose Eye on the Mahoosuc trail, traveling through 1½ miles of woods and ledge. Move down in a northwestward direction on the Goose Eye trail watching for a sharp left turn one mile below the summit. Then pick up an old logging road and in one mile the Success Pond Road and your car.

6. THE OWL
7½ miles round trip, vertical rise 2,630 feet, hiking time 5¾ hours   (Map Key H-5)

One of the many Baxter Park peaks, the Owl provides an outpost between Barren Mt. and Hamlin Peak.

Starting Point   Drive to Katahdin Stream Campground in Baxter State Park. Locate the Hunt trail, part of the AT trail system.

The Hike   Use the Hunt trail to begin the ascent. Travel NE for one mile where the Owl trail bears left. Pass Katahdin Falls, then climb up the steep ridge of the Owl. At 3 miles cross ledges, then at 3½ miles the summit. Return by retracing your route.

7. BALDPATE MOUNTAIN
8 miles round trip, vertical rise 2,700 feet, hiking time 6½ hours   (Map Key D-1)

Baldpate looms over the Grafton Notch arena of mountains. Somewhat remote, she sits unspoiled for the determined hiker.

Starting Point   Travel north on Rt. 26 from Bethel to Newry and North Newry. Approximately 8 miles north of this town watch for the AT signs in Grafton Notch State

Park. There is a small parking area on the west side of Rt. 26. Baldpate rises to the east. The trail west climbs Old Spec (see Advanced Hikes). There is a trail map at the parking area.

The Hike The Appalachian Trail is the main route to Baldpate. Start on east side of Rt. 26 moving up the AT to the Grafton Notch shelter at ¼ mile. Keep the brook near the shelter to your right and climb up behind the lean-to. Parallel the brook on a logging road up the west knob to side trail to Table Rock (.6 mile). This trail leads you to outstanding views. Now back to main trail, head up through some muddy going to West Peak. Hike over to East Peak on the AT for best views. Little Baldpate, Spruce, Table and Hull Mountains make your effort worthwhile.

24 Advanced Hikes

1. **South Turner Mountain**
2. **West Kennebago Mountain**
3. **Saddleback Mountain**
4. **Old Spec**
5. **Mount Abraham**
6. **Mount Katahdin**

1. SOUTH TURNER MOUNTAIN
4 miles round trip, vertical rise 1,630 feet, hiking time 3¼ hours   (Map Key H-6)

North Turner, East Turner and South Turner form a triangle of mountains just east of Mt. Katahdin, with South Turner looking right at Katahdin.

Starting Point I-95 to Medway, west on Rt. 157/11 to Millinocket, NW on the Park Road to the park entrance. Enter and pass through Togue Pond to Roaring Brook Campsite. The trail to South Turner starts here. Make reservations to camp at this site through Baxter State Park, 64 Balsam Drive, Millinocket, ME 04462.

The Hike The trail to South Turner and Russell Pond pair up at the start. Then as Russell turns left, go straight ahead. Bear right at the Sandy Stream Pond trail to reach a boulder field at approximately 1 mile. Cairns mark the trail here. The north summit is reached over open ledges.

2. WEST KENNEBAGO MOUNTAIN
4½ miles round trip, vertical rise 1,800 feet, hiking time 3 hours   (Map Key F-1)

One of the fine hikes in the Rangeley area. West Kennebago is 10 miles from the Canadian border and offers outstanding overlooks.

Starting Point Travel north from Rangeley on Rt. 16 to the Forest Ranger Station at Toothaker Brook, 4½ miles west of Oquossoc. Both maps and fire permits are available here. Then travel west from the station .3 mile on Rt. 16, turn right onto gravel road through Brown Company lands for 2 miles. Bear right and go 2 miles, bear right again onto a good gravel road, the Lincoln Pond Rd. Travel 7 miles, then watch for small sign indicating trail to the fire tower. If you cross the bridge at Little Kennebago Stream, you've gone too far. Be sure to park well off the road since large logging trucks believe the road belongs to them. It does!

The Hike   The trail follows a jeep trail at the beginning, then climbs swiftly over two ridges. At one mile cross several brooks. Follow sign up a steep slope to the warden's camp at 1½ miles. As you climb above the warden's camp you may be able to see the old telephone lines that hook the camp to the tower. The tower is 2¼ miles from the base. Truly superior views of Big Kennebago Lake and surrounding terrain are available here.

Sugarloaf/USA photo.

3. SADDLEBACK MOUNTAIN
10¼ miles round trip, vertical rise 2,450 feet, hiking time 6½ hours   (Map Key F-2)

Saddleback is a good name for this mountain. It spreads over a vast distance and the skyline clearly shows a dip or saddle.

Starting Point   Locate Rt. 4 Farmington to Rangeley. Drive northwest through Phillips and Madrid (pronounced mad'rid). Watch for the Appalachian Trail crossing Rt. 4 approximately 3–4 miles above Smalls Falls. There is a small dirt road here near a red house (it was red!) This can also be located 9 miles east of the Rangeley Inn on Rt. 4. Park off road out of sight of the house. Follow dirt road downhill and over a bridge to link up with the AT.

The Hike   From the AT sign hike over a gravel road past a gravel pit, then over the old tote road which peters out to a trail to Piazza Rock lean-to at 1½ miles. There is a blue blaze trail to the Rock (¼ mile). The Saddleback trail forges straight ahead eastward, then northeast, then tops a ridge, then another ridge before dropping along the west shore of Ethel Pond. Beyond the pond you hike through boggy areas to Mud Pond on your left. As you might guess the travel here is muddy going. Going northwest, easy climbs put you at overlook at Eddy Pond. Continue past the south end of Eddy Pond, bear sharp left along the east shore, climb more steeply now on a worn trail to the ledges. The timberline is reached, then several summits and the trail (left) to the ski slope. This is a good way to get off the mountain quickly if you have an emergency. The main summit and lookout tower are reached at 5 miles.

4. OLD SPEC
5¹/₂ miles round trip, vertical rise 2,730 feet, hiking time 5 hours   (Map Key D-1)

Old Spec is Maine's third highest mountain. Katahdin and Sugarloaf are taller. She sits high overlooking Grafton Notch, which affords a panoramic view of the mountain as it frames the west side of Rt. 26.

Starting Point   From Bethel travel north on Rt. 26. Approximately 8 miles north of North Newry watch for the parking area about 3 miles from Screw Auger Falls in Grafton Notch State Park. The hike starts at the same place as the Baldpate Mt. hike listed in the intermediate hikes.

The Hike   A few pointers. There is a map at the base. Use the route that follows the AT. The old Fire Warden's trail can be climbed but is the steepest in Maine.

Start at Rt. 26 on the Old Spec trail, bear left where Eyebrow trail enters, cross Cascade Brook into two S turns, and along Cascade Brook to the ledges and the Eyebrow. The trail then makes a long loop west and south passing the Link trail ½ mile below the summit (this is return route). Pass the trail and push to Old Spec summit.

Be sure to plan time at the top since a 360° panorama awaits the sturdy hiker. Mahoosuc Notch, the twin peaks of Baldpate, Slide and Dresser Mts. are examples.

Return via the Old Spec trail to the Link (½ mile), turn right at Link, climb down a steep grade to the old cabin site. Cross the clearing, pass close to the brook but to the left (north side). The gradient is very steep so plan your descent accordingly. When you reach Rt. 26, bear left back to your car.

5. MOUNT ABRAHAM
8¼ miles round trip, vertical rise 3,050 feet, hiking time 6 hours   (Map Key F-2)

A slope this is not. A full 4000 feet above sea level! Abraham is an imposing mountain offering every kind of hiking experience.

Starting Point   Arrive in Kingfield via Rt. 27, ¼ mile north of town turn left at the Lumber Company. At 3½ miles bear straight to a point 6 miles from Kingfield. Park by Rapid Stream. Do not try to cross the stream with your vehicle.

The Hike   Cross over Rapid Stream, bear right up the west bank, then westward. Cross Norton Brook, then go west and northwest over a series of feeder brooks to an old warden's cabin. From here plan on a 2,000 foot rise over 1½ miles. The approach to the top is marked by a boulder field, then the summit.

Photo courtesy of Maine Fish & Game

6. MOUNT KATAHDIN
Helon Taylor to the Knife Edge and Baxter Peak, 8½ miles round trip, vertical rise 3,700 feet, hiking time 6½ hours   (Map Key H-6)

Mt. Katahdin is the hiker's dream. On a good day the Helon Taylor trail allows heart-stopping views all the way to the top. Katahdin is also unforgiving for those who stretch their endurance or who climb in unfavorable weather, especially wind and cold. This is a paradise but must be treated with caution.

Starting Point   I-95 to Medway, Rt. 157/11 to Millinocket and the Park Road. Enter the Park and drive to Roaring Brook Campground. Reservations available from Baxter State Park Authority, 64 Balsam Drive, Millinocket, ME 04462.

The Hike   The trail leaves from the parking area. The park rangers ask you to sign *in* on a register and *out* when you leave as a safety measure. Be sure to carry some water, and a sweater or windbreaker even on hot days.

Hike on the Chimney Pond trail for a short way, then turn left onto the Helon Taylor trail. The route is clearly marked and ascends through lower tree growth and rather quickly breaks out into the open. A long spiny ridge points straight to Pamola Peak and requires a scramble over large broken rocks.

On Pamola there are some circular rock shelters like gun emplacements that make a good spot for lunch. The Knife Edge starts from a dip across from Pamola. The climb down from Pamola into the area near the Chimney is sharp and hikers should assist each other here as well as up the other side onto the Knife Edge. The Knife Edge itself is a rough pile of huge broken rocks which can be quite narrow in places. This is not a dangerous place but *is* one where you won't want to read a paper while you're climbing! Across the Knife, continue along the ridge to Baxter Peak. A pile of stones have been stacked to mark the summit. You may return via the same route or continue along the ridge and descend on the Cathedral trail to Chimney Pond and a 3 mile hike from there to Roaring Brook. Cathedral is very steep and difficult going for tired legs.

A somewhat longer but more gentle descent can be found at the Saddle trail along the lip of the Tableland. This also leads to Chimney Pond. These trails will make the round trip distance close to 10 miles, so plan accordingly.

■ Parks and Preserves

Persons planning to use Maine's wild areas for recreation are reminded that services and supplies are frequently many miles away. Many sections of the Appalachian Trail extend above the tree line. Adequate preparations must be made, and caution exercised, before heading into the wilderness.

For more information about these and many other Public Reserved Lands, contact the Information and Education Section, Maine Department of Conservation, Augusta, ME 04333. For more information about the Appalachian Trail, contact the Maine Appalachian Trail Club, Box 283, Augusta, ME 04330.

25 State Parks

Designed to harmonize with mountain, lake and seashore, Maine's State Park System is as varied as the State's landscape. In Maine, State Parks are dedicated to the user's enjoyment; you'll find the men and women who manage them friendly and helpful.

Thirteen parks provide camping accommodations; others offer a range of day use activities, from ocean swimming to wilderness hiking. Reservations at camping areas are not available; however, you may want to call ahead a day or two and obtain information about the likelihood of a vacancy. Some parks have group use areas which require reservations.

Fees for camping and day use vary according to the facilities provided. If you visit day use areas frequently, we suggest purchasing a season pass, which is available by mail from the Bureau of Parks and Recreation headquarters in Augusta or at most State Parks during the regular season.

Rules at Maine's State Parks are simple and intended to protect the site and enhance everyone's enjoyment. Pets are not allowed on beaches or at Sebago Lake State Park. Although most facilities are closed to automobiles for the season after Labor Day, many people continue to enjoy the areas on foot during the fall and winter and are encouraged to do so.

The Allagash Wilderness Waterway is a canoe camper's paradise. This 92 mile corridor of lakes and river is surrounded by a vast commercial forest. If you plan to canoe the Allagash, write the Maine Department of Conservation, Bureau of Parks and Recreation, State House Station #22, Augusta, ME 04333 for more information (See Canoing, River Trips.)

Eben Thomas photo

Aroostook State Park is located on Echo Lake, off U.S. Rt. 1 south of Presque Isle, in the heart of Maine's potato country. Hiking on nearby Quoggy Jo Mountain or trout fishing on Echo Lake are popular local activities. Campsites, a bathhouse, and a beach with a lifeguard are provided in season. Snowmobile and cross-country skiing trails are available in the winter. Tel. (207) 768-8341.

Baxter State Park, a wilderness area of 200,000 acres, is located in the north central section of Maine and can be reached by traveling North on I-95, then west through Millinocket.

There are 46 mountain peaks and ridges, 18 of which are above 3000′. This park is best known as the home of Mt. Katahdin and its Baxter peak at 5267′. 140 miles of trails lead hikers past some of the most spectacular views in Maine. Write to the following address for maps and trail information and campgrounds:

> Baxter State Park
> 64 Balsam Drive
> Millinocket, ME 04462

Bradbury Mountain State Park is six miles from the Freeport Exit, off U.S. 95. A short hike to the mountain top allows a view of Casco Bay. Swings, teeters, horseshoe pit, and a softball field are available to campers and daily visitors. Tel. (207) 688-4712.

Camden Hills State Park is two miles north of Camden on U.S. Rt. 1. You may drive or hike to the summit of Mt. Battie for an excellent view of Camden Harbor, Penobscot Bay and inland lakes and rivers. Mt. Megunticook, highest of the Camden Hills, is an easy climb by foot trail. The park offers 30 miles of hiking trails. A 112-site camping area includes flush toilets and hot showers. Salt and fresh water beaches are nearby. Tel. (207) 236–3109.

Cobscook Bay State Park is located on U.S. Rt. 1, four miles south of Dennysville. "Cobscook" is an Indian name meaning "boiling tide," an apt description of the action of the 24 foot tidal currents in the bay. Many campsites and shelters are on the water's edge, secluded among spruce and fir trees. Boating, golfing, hiking, or day trips to nearby Quoddy Head State Park, Moosehorn National Wildlife Refuge, Franklin D. Roosevelt International Park on Campobello Island in New Brunswick are popular with visitors. Tel. (207) 726–4412.

Crescent Beach State Park is about eight miles from Portland on Rt. 77 in Cape Elizabeth. The park affords bathing in the surf or in the sun, at one of Maine's finest beaches. There are picnic tables and grills, a snack bar, and a bathhouse with shower.

Damariscotta Lake State Park beside Rt. 32 in Jefferson offers a fine sand beach swimming area with a lifeguard, a group use shelter, changing areas, picnic tables, and grills.

Ferry Beach State Park is located on Rt. 9 off Bay View Road between Old Orchard Beach and Camp Ellis in Saco. A stand of tupelo trees, rare at this latitude, can be seen in this 100-acre area, which offers a sweeping view of miles of white sand beaches between the Saco River and Pine Point. A changing room, picnic area, and nature trails are available.

Fort Point State Park off U.S. Rt. 1 in Stockton Springs, on the tip of a peninsula jutting into scenic Penobscot Bay, creates an excellent picnicking or fishing spot. It is adjacent to historic Fort Pownall Memorial. A two hundred foot pier accommodates visitors arriving by boat.

Grafton Notch State Park borders Rt. 26 between Upton and Newry. Several hiking trails dot this spectacular, scenic area at the end of the Mahoosuc Range. The 2,000 mile Appalachian Trail passes through the park on the way to the northern terminus, Mt. Katahdin. Sights include: Screw Auger Falls, Spruce Meadow, Mother Walker Falls, Old Speck Mountain, and Moose Cave. Interpretive panels describe the natural history of the area. Facilities include picnic tables and grills.

Holbrook Island Sanctuary borders Penobscot Bay south of Bucksport in Brooksville. This scenic natural area of upland forests and meadows provides opportunity for hiking and the study and appreciation of nature. There are no developed facilities.

Lake St. George State Park, adjacent to Rt. 3 in Liberty, provides easy access to the shore of a crystal clear, spring fed lake. A day-use area includes a beach with lifeguards and a bathhouse. Campers will find 31 sites, flush toilets and showers. You may launch your boat and fish for bass, salmon, perch, and brook trout. Tel. (207) 589–4255.

Lamoine State Park is located on Rt. 184, eight miles from Ellsworth. Located on Frenchman's Bay, the park provides camping and picnicking. A boat launching ramp is available. Acadia National Park on Mt. Desert Island is nearby. Tel. (207) 667–4778.

Lily Bay State Park is about eight miles north of Greenville on the east shore of 40-mile long Moosehead Lake. Beautifully located campsites, many along the shore, are well-spaced, wooded and add to the feeling of the back-country. Moosehead is a lake famous for brook trout, salmon and lake trout (togue). The park offers two fine boat launching sites with berths. A hiking trail is available. Tel. (207) 695-2700.

Moose Point State Park on U.S. Rt. 1 between Belfast and Searsport provides refuge from busy Route One for a cook-out or picnic. Relax in an evergreen grove or open field and enjoy the Penobscot Bay panorama.

Mount Blue State Park is about ten miles from Wilton off Rt. 156 in Weld. Camping, a sand beach with bathhouse, boat launching, an amphitheater and recreation hall are among the features of the Webb Lake area. The nearby Center Hill Area provides a scenic picnic spot and a nature trail. An interpretive naturalist leads scheduled hikes from the camping area. Adirondack shelters are available for large group use and canoes may be rented. Tel. (207) 585-2347.

Peacock Beach State Park is just off Rt. 201 on Pleasant Pond in Richmond, about 10 miles from Augusta. A beautiful small sand beach and swimming area with lifeguards make this an ideal spot for a family picnic.

Peaks-Kenny State Park is nestled in the mountains on the shore of Sebec Lake, at the end of Rt. 153 about six miles from Dover-Foxcroft. The park offers camping, flush toilets, hot water showers, and well-spaced sites in a woodland setting. A lifeguard, picnic area and bathhouse with showers are found at the beach, which is used by campers and day use visitors. Special features such as hiking and amphitheater programs add more variety to this scenic spot. Tel. (207) 564-2003.

Photo by Ken Grey, courtesy of Maine Fish & Game Department.

Popham Beach State Park—take Rt. 209 fourteen miles from Bath to Phippsburg and follow park signs to this spacious sand beach. Near old Fort Popham, site of the first attempt by the English to colonize New England.

Quoddy Head State Park is four miles off Rt. 189 at Lubec. The eastern-most point of land and lighthouse in the United States is adjacent to the park. The scenic trail is a photographer's delight with rock cliffs rising spectacularly from the ocean 80 feet below.

Rangeley Lake State Park can be reached from Rumford via Rt. 17 or from Farmington via Rt. 4. Located in an area famous for trout and landlocked salmon fishing, photographers will find some of the most beautiful scenery in the state in this region of mountains and lakes. You will find a concrete boat launching ramp with floats, hot showers and well spaced campsites among the fragrant spruce and fir trees. Tel. (207) 864–3858.

Range Ponds State Park is just off the Empire Road in Poland. The Empire Road is approached from Rt. 122; take Rt. 26 north from Gray, or Rt. 202 south from Lewiston which will connect with Rt. 122. Range Ponds is a day use park with facilities for picnicking, has a ballfield, and a swimming area with lifeguards.

Reid State Park is reached by traveling Rt. 127 from Woolwich, fourteen miles to park entrance. Nearly a mile and a half of sand beaches, dunes, marshes, ledges, and ocean, plus a warm salt water pond for swimming make Reid one of Maine's most popular saltwater parks. There are bathhouses with fresh water showers, fireplaces, snack bar, and a modest parking area.

Roque Bluffs State Park in the town of Roque Bluffs about six miles off U.S. Rt. 1, is a unique day-use area providing both fresh and salt water swimming. There is a pebble beach on the ocean and a fresh water pond. Facilities include tables, grills, changing areas with vault toilets, and a children's playground.

Scarboro Beach State Park may be reached by traveling about three miles on Rt. 207 south from U.S. Rt. 1 in the Town of Scarborough. The area includes a small, sandy beach with a mixture of dunes, marshes and ocean surf.

Drinking water, changing rooms, and limited parking are available.

Sebago Lake State Park is located off U.S. Rt. 302 between Naples and South Casco. The day use area features extensive sand beaches, tables, grills, a boat ramp, lifeguards, and bathhouses. A camping area offers excellent beaches near the campsites. Flush toilets and hot showers are available. An amphitheater with scheduled programs and Ranger conducted hikes on nature trails are offered. The clear water of Sebago Lake provides Portland's water supply and supports a high quality fresh water sport fishery for salmon and togue. Songo Lock is nearby and permits a boat trip up the Songo River to Long Lake. Tel. (207) 693–6613 between June 20th and Labor Day. Before June 20th and after Labor Day; Tel. (207) 693–6231.

Swan Lake State Park on the shores of its namesake in the Swanville area is one of Maine's newest parks. Follow signs from Rt. 141 north of Swanville for excellent swimming and picnicking facilities.

Two Lights State Park is off Maine Route 77 in Cape Elizabeth. Picnic or stroll along the rocky headland and enjoy a marvelous view of Casco Bay, the open Atlantic and crashing surf, while lobstermen haul their traps off shore. Picnic tables and grills are available. Crescent Beach State Park is only a half mile away.

Warren Island State Park, a spruce covered island in Penobscot Bay, offers docking and mooring facilities on the lee side for protection. Sleep aboard your boat, or moor it and come ashore to picnic or camp in a park shelter or your own tent. Contact Camden Hills State Park for information about transportation to Warren Island. Facilities

132

include ten camping sites, two Adirondack shelters, and fresh drinking water.

Wolf Neck Woods State Park on Wolf Neck Road south of Freeport is dedicated to nature interpretation and appreciation. Guided natural history tours start at the picnic area and follow rustic shoreline hiking trails. Scenic frontage on Casco Bay and the Harraseeket River. Follow Bow Street from Freeport to Wolf Neck Road.

Sugarloaf/USA photo.

State Parks

	STATE PARKS	LOCATION	BATHING	BOAT LAUNCHING	FISHING	CAMPING	HIKING	PICNICKING	SNOWMOBILING	SNACK BAR	DUMPING STATION	DATES
1	Aroostook	Presque Isle	✔	✔	✔	✔	✔	✔	✔			5/15-10/15
2	Bradbury Mountain	Pownal				✔	✔	✔				5/15-11/1
3	Camden Hills	Camden				✔	✔	✔	✔		✔	5/15-11/1
4	Cobscook Bay	Dennysville		✔	✔	✔	✔	✔	✔		✔	5/15-10/15
5	Crescent Beach	Cape Elizabeth	✔		✔			✔		✔		5/30-9/30
6	Damariscotta Lake	Jefferson	✔		✔			✔				5/30-LD
7	Ferry Beach	Saco River	✔			✔		✔				5/30-LD
8	Fort Point	Stockton Springs			✔		✔					5/30-LD
9	Grafton Notch	Upton & Newry			✔		✔	✔				5/30-10/15
10	Holbrook Is. Sanctuary	Brooksville					✔	✔				5/30-11/1
11	Lake St. George	Liberty	✔	✔	✔	✔		✔	✔		✔	5/15-10/15
12	Lamoine	Ellsworth		✔	✔	✔		✔				5/15-10/15
13	Lily Bay	Greenville	✔	✔	✔	✔		✔	✔		✔	IO-10/15
14	Moose Point	Searsport						✔				5/30-10/15
15	Mt. Blue	Weld	✔	✔	✔	✔	✔	✔	✔		✔	5/30-10/15
16	Peacock Beach	Richmond	✔		✔			✔				5/30-LD
17	Peaks-Kenny	Dover-Foxcroft	✔		✔	✔	✔	✔			✔	5/30-9/30
18	Popham Beach	Phippsburg	✔		✔			✔				4/15-11/30
19	Quoddy Head	Lubec					✔	✔				5/30-10/30
20	Rangeley Lake	Rangeley	✔	✔	✔	✔		✔	✔		✔	IO-10/15
21	Range Ponds	Poland	✔	✔	✔			✔				5/30-10/15
22	Reid	Georgetown	✔		✔			✔		✔		4/15-12/15
23	Roque Bluffs	Roque Bluffs	✔		✔			✔				5/15-10/15
24	Scarborough Beach	Scarborough	✔		✔			✔				5/30-LD
25	Sebago Lake	Naples	✔	✔	✔	✔		✔		✔	✔	5/1-10/15
26	Swan Lake	Belfast	✔		✔			✔				5/30-LD
27	Two Lights	Cape Elizabeth			✔			✔				4/15-12/1
28	Warren Island	Islesboro	✔		✔	✔	✔					5/30-9/30
29	Wolf Neck Woods	Freeport					✔	✔	✔			5/30-LD
30	Allagash Wilderness Waterway		✔	✔	✔			✔	✔			None
31	Baxter Park		✔			✔	✔	✔	✔	✔		See pg. 126

LD = Labor Day
IO = Ice Out

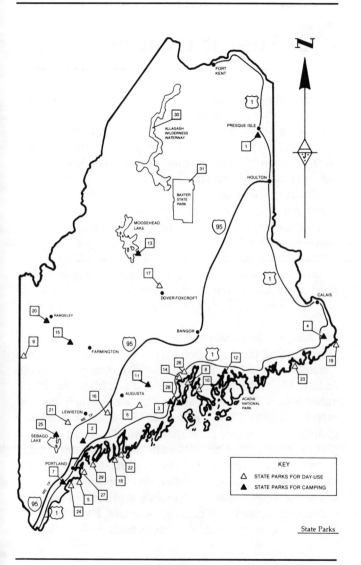

N

FORT
KENT

PRESQUE ISLE

30
ALLAGASH
WILDERNESS
WATERWAY

31

BAXTER
STATE
PARK

HOULTON

95

MOOSEHEAD
LAKE

13

17

DOVER-FOXCROFT

CALAIS

20   RANGELEY

9   15

FARMINGTON

95

BANGOR

1

4

11   14   26   8   12

16   28   10   19

AUGUSTA

21   LEWISTON   3   23

6

2   ACADIA
25   NATIONAL
SEBAGO   PARK
LAKE

PORTLAND

7   29

22

18

5   27

24

1

KEY

△ STATE PARKS FOR DAY-USE

▲ STATE PARKS FOR CAMPING

State Parks

26 Historic Sites

A sampling of Maine's rich historical heritage has been preserved and interpreted by the Bureau of Parks and Recreation at eighteen important historic memorials. You are invited to explore old forts which protected America's waterways during the Revolution and Civil War, visit a blast furnace and charcoal kiln deep in Maine's colorful wildlands or spend an afternoon at a magnificent replica of a Revolutionary War hero's mansion. Many areas offer picnic facilities; brief printed histories of some areas may be purchased on site.

Most memorials are open seven days a week between 10:00 a.m. and 6:00 p.m. from Memorial Day to Labor Day. After Labor Day, visitors are welcome at the sites, although access at some may be limited to outdoor areas.

The Arnold Trail stretches 194 miles from Fort Popham, at the mouth of the Kennebec River, north and west to the Canadian border at Coburn Gore. It traces the route followed by Colonel Benedict Arnold and his troops in the autumn of 1775 on the Maine Portion of their historic march to Quebec. The march ended in an unsuccessful attempt to take Quebec from the British. There are 33 interpretive panels at nine different sites along the route: Popham, Hallowell, Skowhegan, Solon, Moscow, Stratton, Sarampus, Chain of Ponds, and Coburn Gore. Some of the buildings passed by Arnold's men are still standing today, including Fort Western in Augusta, Fort Halifax in Winslow, and the old Pownalborough Courthouse in Dresden.

Colonial Pemaquid is situated on a point of land at the mouth of the Pemaquid River in Bristol. Extensive archeological excavations have unearthed 14 foundations of 17th and 18th century structures. A museum displays hundreds of artifacts found on the site, dating from prehistoric times to the colonial period. Musket balls, old coins, pottery, and early hardware are among items of interest. While there, you can visit a reconstruction of Fort William Henry, adjacent to the settlement site. Drive four miles on Rt. 129 from Damariscotta, then take Rt. 130 for nine miles, bear right one mile.

Eagle Island, about three miles off the coast of Harpswell, was the summer home of North Pole explorer, Admiral Robert E. Peary. The island is equipped with a pier which makes visitation possible throughout the summer for picnickers, nature enthusiasts, and history buffs. Contact the Maine Bureau of Parks and Recreation for information concerning boats for hire which provide transportation to the island.

Fort Edgecomb was built to protect picturesque Wiscasset, once the most important shipping center north of Boston. This octagonal 1808 blockhouse and restored fortifications overlook the Sheepscot River, where harbor seals are often seen. Take U.S. Rt. 1 south to the Edgecomb end of the Wiscasset bridge, then next right.

Fort George in historic Castine, originally built by the British in 1779, is an intact earthwork dating from the Revolution. Interpretive panels describe this fort which was erected in a village variously occupied throughout the colonial period by the English, French, Dutch and Americans. Take Rt. 166 into Castine.

Fort Halifax, the oldest blockhouse still standing in the United States, was built in 1754. The blockhouse, which is at the confluence of the Sebasticook and Kennebec Rivers, was part of a larger fortification used as a way station for Colonel Benedict Arnold's expedition through the Maine wilderness to Quebec in 1775. Travel one mile south of Winslow-Waterville bridge on U.S. Rt. 201.

Fort William Henry in Bristol was originally built in 1692. The existing replica of this fortification is open to visitors. An earlier fort on this site was erected about 1630 to defend the settlement against pirates. The fort replicated in the present structure was built for defense against the Indians and was destroyed by the French in 1696. A museum, which is part of the Colonial Pemaquid Restoration, contains many artifacts, portraits, and maps related to the original fort. Drive four miles on Rt. 129 from Damariscotta, then take Rt. 130 for nine miles, bear right one mile.

John Paul Jones Memorial commemorates the nearby site where in 1777 the U.S.S. Ranger was built and launched. On this ship, Jones received the first salute given by a foreign power to a man-of-war flying the Stars and Stripes. Located on U.S. Rt. 1 in the center of Kittery.

Katahdin Iron Works is the site of a once thriving iron works built in 1843. A restored blast furnace and charcoal kiln remind visitors of an effort that produced nearly 2000 tons of raw iron annually for half a century. Charcoal was made in 14 kilns consuming 10,000 cords of wood a year. From Rt. 11, drive five miles north of Brownville Junction, then take gravel road six miles to "K.I."

Fort Kent blockhouse was constructed in 1839 for the bloodless Aroostook Border War and named for Maine's

Governor Edward Kent. This site was part of a more extensive fortification and contains a small museum of lumbering and Indian artifacts. Off U.S. Rt. 1 in the Town of Fort Kent.

Fort Knox, the second largest fort in the United States, located in Prospect, is a splendid example of granite craftsmanship. Construction was started in 1844 as part of the defense for the Aroostook War and continued for twenty years. The substantial structure, including spiral staircases of granite, has remained in excellent shape for over a century. The narrows of the Penobscot River provide a strategic site for this fortification, which was manned during the Civil and Spanish American Wars. On Rt. 174, just off U.S. Rt. 1 west of the Waldo-Hancock Bridge.

Fort McClary is an 1846 blockhouse on the site of fortifications of 1715, 1776, and 1808. Initial use of this site in the early 18th century was to protect Massachusetts vessels from taxation by the New Hampshire Colony. Later use was made of this site during the Revolution, the War of 1812, the Civil War, and the Spanish-American War. Leave Turnpike and U.S. Rt. 1 at rotary in Kittery, then travel south two and a half miles on Kittery Point Road (Rt. 103). Picnic facilities are available.

Montpelier is a handsome replica of the original mansion built in 1793 and contains most of the original possessions of Major General and Mrs. Henry Knox. One of the great heroes of the Revolutionary War, at age 31 Knox became the youngest Major General of the time and is credited with planning all the battles won by General Washington. After the Revolution, he served for ten years as the first Secretary of War, during which time he built "Montpelier." One mile east of Thomaston on U.S. Rt. 1.

Fort O'Brien (Fort Machias), built in 1775 and destroyed by the British in the same year, was refortified in 1777 and destroyed once again by the British in 1814. Well-preserved earthworks which overlook Machias Bay were erected for a battery of guns in 1863. The first naval engagement of the Revolution was fought offshore in 1775, five days before the Battle at Bunker Hill. Travel five miles from Machias on Rt. 92.

Fort Popham is a semi-circular granite fort built in 1861 for use during the Civil War. Modifications were made and the

Photo by Tom Carbone, courtesy of Maine Fish & Game Department.

fort used again in the Spanish American War and World War I. Historical records conclude that fortifications, probably wooden, existed here and protected the Kennebec settlements during the Revolutionary War and the War of 1812. It was nearby that the English made their first attempt to colonize New England in 1607. The fort is 15 miles from Bath on Maine Rt. 209.

Fort Pownall was located and built in 1759 by Massachusetts Royal Governor Thomas Pownall. To prevent its being taken intact by American patriots, the British burned the wooden fort in 1775 and again in 1779. Only earthworks remain. The Fort is part of Fort Point State Park. Leave U.S. Rt. 1 at Stockton Springs and follow signs.

Songo Lock is located midway between Long Lake and Sebago Lake on the Songo River in Naples and was first constructed in 1830. Built of stone masonry with wooden gates, the original lock was 90 feet long and 26 feet wide. The Sebago Improvement Company increased the size of the lock to 110 feet by 28 feet when they rebuilt it in 1911. The Lock, which is adjacent to Sebago Lake State Park, provides passage between Sebago Lake and Long Lake for recreational boaters.

Vaughan Woods, on the banks of Salmon Falls River, has a rich historical heritage. In 1634, here at "Cow Cove," the first cows in this part of the country were landed from the ship "The Pied Cow." Much of this 250 acre tract is forest, with picnic facilities, nature trails, and markers identifying the woodland flora. Off Rt. 91, one half mile south of South Berwick, then west opposite High School, one mile to entrance.

HISTORIC SITES—QUICK REFERENCE

Historic Sites	Location	Acreage	Map Index	Snack Bar	Scenic Road	Picnicking	Boat Launch	Fishing	Fee Charged	Hiking	Opening/Closing Dates
Arnold Trail	Popham to Coburn Gore				•	•					
Colonial Pemaquid (Ft. Wm. Henry)	Bristol	8	C-4	•		•	•	•	•		May 30 through Labor Day
Eagle Island	S. Harpswell	17	C-3			•					June 20 through Labor Day
Fort Edgecomb	N. Edgecomb	3	C-4			•					May 30 through Labor Day
Fort George	Castine	3	D-6			•		•	•		May 30 through Labor Day
Fort Halifax	Winslow	0.75	E-4								May 30 through Labor Day

										All Year
John Paul Jones	Kittery	2	A-1							
Katahdin Iron Works	T6 R9	17.8	G-5		•					May 30 through Labor Day
Fort Kent	Fort Kent	3	K-6							May 30 through Labor Day
Fort Knox	Prospect	124	E-6		•			•		May 1 to November 1
Fort McClary	Kittery Point	27	A-1		•			•		May 30 to October 10
Montpelier	Thomaston	6.5	C-5					•		May 30 to September 1
Fort O'Brien (Fort Machias)	Machiasport	2	E-9		•					May 30 through Labor Day
Fort Popham	Popham Beach	7	C-3		•		•	•		May 30 through Labor Day
Songo Lock	Naples	1.35	C-1		•			•		June 15 through Labor Day
Vaughan Woods	S. Berwick	250	A-1						•	May 30 through Labor Day

27 Public Lands

The Bureau of Public Lands is a multiple-use land management agency responsible for the administration of 400,000 acres of Public Reserved Land in the State of Maine. These lands are managed for a variety of resource values, including timber production, recreation and wildlife. Recreation is keyed particularly to primitive, dispersed types of outdoor activities such as camping, fishing, and hiking.

Unpaved private roads provide access to many of these backcountry recreation areas. *Drivers are cautioned to yield the right-of-way to logging trucks at all times.*

The Bigelow Preserve

The 30,000-acre Bigelow Preserve, which embraces Flagstaff Lake in western Maine, constitutes a unique patchwork of mountains, forests, and lakes established by popular referendum and administered jointly by the Bureau of Parks and Recreation, Bureau of Public Lands, and Department of Inland Fisheries and Wildlife. Hiking along the Appalachian Trail is one of the most visible recreational activities on this tract; however, fishing, swimming, and camping (authorized Forest Service campsites) are also available. Access to the Bigelow Preserve is gained via Rt. 27 out of New Portland north to Stratton Brook, where a gravel road—marked "Appalachian Trail"—turns to the northeast.   (Map Key F-2)

Gardner-Deboulie

The Gardner-Deboulie Management Unit, located in Township 15, Range 9 WELS, Aroostook County, represents 20,000 acres of rugged mountain peaks, small wilderness lakes, and hiking trails. Visitors to this area will delight in the variety of this primitive landscape, the stark contrasts between mountains and surrounding forests, and the quiet sense of discovery, as each woodland path anticipates another isolated shore. Access to this unit is gained via a private road, extending northwest off Rt. 11 out of Portage. In addition to several primitive campsites visitors may also stay at commercially operated camps in the area. (Map Key J-6)

Gero Island

Gero Island—and much of the surrounding countryside—is accessible by water only. A 3,000 acre tract at the head of Chesuncook Lake, Gero Island is located in Township 5 Range 13 (Piscataquis County). It is situated close to historic Chesuncook Village and serves as a convenient stop-over for recreationists canoeing the West Branch of the Penobscot River or traveling south along the Allagash Wilderness Waterway. There are primitive campsites on both the mainland and the island and a sporting camp at Chesuncook Village. Launching sites are accessible at both the north and south ends of the lake via private logging roads, which extend to the northwest from Rt. 11 out of Millinocket. (Map Key H-4)

The Mahoosucs

The Mahoosuc Mountains of western Maine extend across Riley and Grafton Townships in two units—separated by Rt. 26 and Grafton Notch State Park. Along this mountainous terrain, some elevations rising over 3,500 feet, occurs some of the most challenging hiking within the northeastern segment of the Appalachian Trail. This rugged setting is characterized by steep gorges and picturesque waterfalls, glacial tarns and cirques, and delicately colorful subalpine heaths. Accessible via Rt. 26 out of Bethel,

visitors will find three lean-to shelters and several primitive
campsites—all developed and maintained by the Appalachian Mountain Club in cooperation with the Bureau of
Public Lands.   (Map Key E-1)

Scraggly Lake
Scraggly Lake dominates the 10,000-acre management unit
which bears its name. Located in the south half of
Township 7 Range 8 (Penobscot County), this irregularly-
shaped body of water offers boaters and fishermen alike
opportunities for both discovery and exploration in many
small coves and around numerous islands. It is also possible
to hike into the smaller and more remote Ireland Pond to
the northwest. There is a four-unit Maine Forest Service
campground and boat-launching ramp on the south shore
of the lake. Access to this unit may be gained via the Old
Scraggly Lake Road, which extends north from the Grand
Lake Road out of Shin Pond (Mount Chase).   (Map Key
H-7)

28 Wildlife Areas

The Brownfield Wildlife Management Area is a 5,600 acre
preserve located 1.5 miles northeast of East Brownfield off
Rt. 160. There are 1,540 acres of inland freshwater
wetlands, and emphasis is on waterfowl nesting and feeding
areas. Camping is available, along with a boat launching
facility.

The Swan Island W.M.A. consists of over 1,750 acres
located along the Kennebec River near Merrymeeting Bay
and Richmond. Over 500 acres are coastal freshwater
wetlands, the remainder of the preserve consisting of

forest, goose pasture, and inland wetlands. Camping and day-use visits to Swan and Little Swan Islands are controlled by permit (fee charged) available from Inland Fish & Wildlife, Augusta, ME 04333. The area is a major stop for resting and feeding during the Canada goose migration.

The Scarborough W.M.A. contains over 3,000 acres located in the towns of Scarborough, Saco, and Old Orchard Beach. Over 1,600 acres of wetlands (fresh and salt, coastal and inland) provide habitat for many bird species, some found nowhere else in Maine. The Scarborough Marsh Nature Center, Rt. 9, Scarborough, is a mini-museum operated by the Audubon Society, providing marsh hikes and canoe rentals in season.

OTHER WILDLIFE MANAGEMENT AREAS

Name	Location	Size*	Description
Chesterville	Chesterville	466	inland freshwater wetlands
Fahi Pond	Embden	297	inland freshwater wetlands
Frye Mt.	Montville	5,176	upland game and furbearers
Great Works	Edmunds	640	inland freshwater wetlands
Jonesboro	Jonesboro	713	upland game, deer, 31 acres inland freshwater wetlands
Madawaska	Palmyra	295	inland freshwater wetlands
Manuel	Hodgdon	4,994	upland game inland freshwater wetlands boat launch, swimming
H. Mendall	Frankfort Prospect	221	coastal wetlands, fresh and salt
Mercer Bog	Mercer	95	inland freshwater wetlands
Newfield	Shapleigh Newfield	4,556	upland game and furbearers inland freshwater wetlands
Old Farm Pond	Maxfield Howland	1,200	inland freshwater wetlands
Orange River	Whiting	588	inland freshwater wetlands
Ruffingham	Montville Searsmont	610	inland freshwater wetlands

(cont'd)

*(acres)

OTHER WILDLIFE MANAGEMENT AREAS (*cont'd*)

Name	Location	Size*	Description
St. Albans	St. Albans	542	inland freshwater wetlands
Sandy Point	Stockton Springs	543	inland freshwater wetlands
Scammon	Eastbrook Franklin	1,813	inland freshwater wetlands
R. Waldo Tyler	Rockland Thomaston	533	upland, woodland coastal wetland

*(acres)

29 Nature Preserves

These areas have been set aside to preserve native Maine wildlife. They have excellent educational opportunities. Most have trails, and hunting and trapping are not permitted. The *Maine Audubon Society,* Gilson Farm, Falmouth, ME 04105 would be a good source to follow up for additional information or the Chamber of Commerce in the town where they are located.

Preserve	What you are most likely to see	Town	Map Key
Arey's Neck Woods	Island vista, marsh, reach by ferry, southeast end Island	Vinalhaven Island 04863	C-6
Armbrust Hill	Abandoned quarry, picnic area, reach by ferry, south end Island	Vinalhaven Island 04863	C-6

Preserve	What you are most likely to see	Town	Map Key
Back Bay Sanctuary	Shore birds, black duck inside city limits	Portland 04101	BC-2
Basket Island	Forested Casco Bay Island coves for swimming, reach by boat	Cumberland 04110	BC-2
Baxter Woods	Bird sanctuary, 30 acres	Portland 04101	BC-2
Birdscare Sanctuary	Bird Sanctuary, 20 acres	Ellsworth 04605	E-7
Blagden Preserve	Saltwater shoreline, 110 acres, conifers	Bar Harbor 04609	D-7
Crockett Cove	100 acres on saltwater, has nature trail	Stonington 04681	D-6
Douglas Mt. Preserve	Good views from summit, 169 acres	Sebago 04075	F-4
East Point Sanctuary	Audubon Sanctuary, 30 acres, pebble beaches	Biddeford 04005	B-2
Gilson Farm	Me. Audubon Society Headquarters, 70 acres, trails	Falmouth 04105	C-2
The Hermitage	Growth of old pine, on trail to Gulf Hagas.	Brownville Jct. 04415	G-5
Hirham Nature Study	Trails along Saco River, tours available, hunting permitted here	Baldwin	C-1
Holbrook Island	State owned, hiking along saltwater shore	Brookville 04617	D-6

149

Preserve	What you are most likely to see	Town	Map Key
Josephine Newman (Wildlife Sanctuary)	Nature walks on trails over ledges, saltwater	Georgetown 04548	C-3
Lanes Island Preserve	Wave cut coastline, saltwater trails, ferry to Vinalhaven, road to preserve, south end Island	Vinalhaven 04863	C-6
Mast Landing	Audubon Sanctuary, trails on tidal river east of Freeport	Freeport 04032	C-3
Moosehorn Nat'l Wildlife Refuge	22,665 acres, bogs, marshes, forest, located southwest of Calais, borders St. Croix River	Baring 04619	F-9
Morse Mt. Preserve	Salt marsh, sandy beach, 600 acres	Phippsburg 04562	C-3
Osborn Finch Preserve	11 acres forest and shoreline of Medomac River	Waldoboro 04572	D-4
Prout's Neck Bird Sanctuary	Nature trails, no parking, use bikes	Scarborough 04074	B-2
Rachel Carson Nat'l Wildlife Preserve	Salt marsh, birds	Wells 04090	B-2

Preserve	What you are most likely to see	Town	Map Key
Rachel Carson Salt Pond Preserve	Small tidal salt pond, 78 acres	Bristol 04539	C-4
Robert P. T. Coffin Wildflower Reservation	Nature Sanctuary, trails thru forest	Woolwich 04579	C-3
Scarborough Marsh Nature Center	3,000 acres, small museum, largest Maine salt marsh, canoe trips for birders	Scarborough 04074	B-2
Ship Harbor Nature Trail	Pink granite ledges, good views, saltwater	Southwest Harbor 04679	D-7
Steve Powell Refuge & Wildlife Mgt. Area	On Swan Island in Kennebec River, good chance to see deer, camping, tours, 1,753 acres	Richmond 04357 (nearest town)	D-3
Steep Falls Preserve	200' waterfalls, Mt. stream, swimming cold!	Newry 04261	D-1
Thorncrag Bird Sanctuary	One of largest bird sanctuaries in New England	Lewiston 04240	D-2,3
Todd Wildlife Sanctuary	Audubon nature study on Hog Island	Bremen, 04572	C-4
Vaughan Woods Memorial	Historic Indian trail included, wooded	So. Berwick 03901	A-1

■ Camping

30 Remote Campsites

Maine's forests and woodlands cover a vast 17,749,000 acres stretching from Kittery to Allagash. Most of the canoeing, fishing, and camping country is owned by large paper companies.

They have established the multiple use concept so the public can have access to these lands for recreation while they pursue the profitable aspects of timber harvesting. A network of roads have been built by these companies and most are open to the public or open by permit. Their logical concern is fire. The state, in cooperation with these companies, has established *two* kinds of campsites.

The first is called an "authorized site" and is marked by a large white sign which says "Campsite authorized by Maine Forest Service." At these locations you may camp overnight and kindle a fire without a permit.

The second is the so-called "Fire Permit Site." These are usually in areas where there is greater danger of forest fires. *Forest rangers* can issue "permits" to build fires in these marginal areas depending on the weather.

Note: Maine law allows you to build an open wood or charcoal fire outdoors or within a collapsible shelter at any of these Authorized Campsites at any time without an out-of-door fire permit. This rule applies during a Governor's ban on outdoor fires. In addition, *permits are not necessary* for the use of portable stoves which are fueled with LP gas, gasoline, or sterno.

Now with all of that, what should you do?

Maine has four Regional Districts as shown on the map.

The Regional Rangers can issue a permit by mail if you state date, location of trip and number in your party. If they do not issue the permit they will refer you to either a District Ranger or Forest Ranger who can do so. You should call just prior to your trip to be sure weather conditions still make your permit valid!

Northern Region

Wallace Townsend,
  Regional Ranger
Maine Forest Service
Island Falls, ME 04747
Tel. (207) 463-2214

Western Region

Vaughn Thornton,
  Regional Ranger
Maine Forest Service
P.O. Box 1107
Greenville, ME 04441
Tel. (207) 695-3721

Southern Region

George Hill,
  Regional Ranger
Maine Forest Service
West Paris, ME 04289
Tel. (207) 674-2442

(**Note:** No fire permit
sites in this area
except for Saco River)

Eastern Region

Roger Milligan,
  Regional Ranger
Maine Forest Service
Box 415
Old Town, ME 04468
Tel. (207) 827-2079

NORTH MAINE WOODS

The North Maine Woods is a large tract of land, about 2½ million acres, held in private ownership and managed for timber harvesting. Hunting, fishing, boating, and camping are allowed. Access to the land is closely controlled by gates in many areas, however, and fees are charged.

Information about the North Maine Woods may be obtained by writing to North Maine Woods, Box 382, Ashland, ME 04732.

Maine residents are charged $2 per day, $3.50 per night camping, $10 for season day use, and $15 for all-purpose season registration. Sporting camp visitors are charged $4 per round trip. People over age 70 (Maine resident) are allowed free use.

Non-residents are charged $3.50 per day, $4.50 per night camping, and $25 for season day use registration. Non-resident sporting camp visitors are charged $6 per round trip (max. fee, $25).

Passage to the Allagash Wilderness is treated as a single day use for fee purposes. Passage through any checkpoint after hours is $5.

Fees subject to change. To verify call (207) 435–6213.

Check Points *Telos, Oxbow* and *Fish River* are open 6 a.m. to 10 p.m. daily. In October and November the hours are 5 a.m. to 9 p.m. *St. Francis, Allagash, Dickey, Little Black,* and *Estcourt* are open daily from 5 a.m. to 9 p.m.

Six Mile Checkpoint is open 24 hours a day. *St. Pamphile* 6 a.m. to 8 p.m. (closed Sunday). *Musquacook* 8 a.m. to 8 p.m.

Caucomgomoc Checkpoint is a control gate, and passage is allowed only to Baker Lake for St. John River canoeists and to the Caucomgomoc Campsites. It is open 6 a.m. to 6 p.m.

Daaquam Checkpoint is open Mondays 5 a.m. to 1 p.m. and Tuesday to Friday 6 a.m. to 2 p.m. It is closed Saturday, Sunday, and holidays.

When using the border gates, the hours of American Customs must be considered. *Customs* is open Mondays from 5 a.m. to 1 p.m., Tuesday through Friday from 6 a.m. to 2 p.m. Estcourt opens 5 a.m. to 1 p.m. on Monday and Thursday. *All gates are closed Saturday, Sunday, and holidays.*

Canadian Customs Hours *St. Aurelie,* Monday to Friday, 9 a.m. to 5 p.m.; *Daaquam,* Monday 7 a.m. to 3 p.m., Tuesday 9 a.m. to 5 p.m., Wednesday 9 a.m. to 5 p.m., Thursday 10 a.m. to 6 p.m., Friday 9 a.m. to 5 p.m.; *St. Pamphile,* Monday to Friday 9 a.m. to 5 p.m.; *Estcourt,* Monday to Friday, 9 a.m. to 5 p.m.

Since this all can be quite confusing I suggest you call North Maine Woods, Tel. (207) 435-6213. They will help you be sure of clearing all gates.

Campsites The North Maine Woods is not like most camping areas. The campsites are primitive and well spread out. In most cases the amenities are a fireplace and space for a tent. It is definitely primitive camping.

The maximum length of stay at any campsite in the North Maine Woods is two weeks. Trailers, tents, or other equipment cannot be stored at the campsites.

Camping Permits Camping permits for authorized North Maine Woods campsites are issued at the checkpoints. Those wishing to camp at locations other than these campsites must have a fire permit from the Maine Forest Service. (See Remote Campsites p. 152.)

Fires Dead and down wood can be used for campfires. The fireplace provided is the only place fires may be built at authorized campsites. Moving or building a fireplace is not allowed. When using a fire permit campsite, use an existing fireplace if available.

Maps *North Maine Woods* produces an exceptionally fine map of their region which can be obtained by writing to:

> North Maine Woods
> P.O. Box 382
> Ashland, ME 04732
> Tel. (207) 435-6213

31 Campgrounds

Campgrounds give Maine vacationers unique experiences. Some are remote, quiet places where nature has the front seat. Others are closer to the hub of urban life providing entertainment for young and old.

Each campground listed below belongs to the Maine Campground Owners Association. A complete booklet with additional information may be obtained from them at 655 Main Street, Lewiston, ME 04240.

X = available at campground   D = Dryers only
N = available within 1 mile of MD = Memorial Day weekend
   campground   LD = Labor Day
E = Electricity only   CD = Columbus Day

1—SOUTHERN COAST

Campground	Town	Zip	Phone	Water & Electric	Sewer	Pumping/Dump	Store	Laundry	Rec. Hall	Swimming	Boating	Fishing	Pets Allowed	No. of Sites	Season Dates	Map Key
Bayley's Campground	Scarborough	04074	883-6043	X	X	X	X	X	X	X	X	X		300	5/15-10/1	B-2
Beach Acres Park	Wells	04090	646-5612	X	X	X	X	X	X	X	N	N	X	65	MD-LD	A-1
Beaver Dam Campground	Berwick	03901	698-1985	X		X	X	N	X	X	X	X	X	42	5/15-9/15	B-1
Big Skye Acres	Pownal	04069	688-4147	X	X	X	X	X	X	X	N	X		80	5/1-10/1	C-2
Camp Eaton	York Harbor	03911		X	X	X	N	N	X	N	N	N	X	105	5/01-10/01	A-1
Cape Neddick Campground	Cape Neddick	03902	363-4366	X		X	X	X		X	X	X	X	80	5/15-10/01	A-1
Dixon's Campground	Cape Neddick	03902	363-2131	E			X	D						100	5/18-9/3	A-1
Flagg's Tent & Trailer Park	York Beach	03910	363-5050	X	X	X	N	N	N	N	N	N		90	6/15-9/15	A-1
Flying Point Campground	Freeport	04032	865-4569	X		X				X	X	X	X	30	5/01-10/15	C-3
Gregoires Campground	Wells	04090	646-3711	X	X	X	X		X				X	100	5/15-9/15	B-2
Hid'n Pines Campground	Old Orchard Bch	04064	934-2352	X	X	X	X	N		X	N	N	X	195	5/15-9/15	B-2

1—SOUTHERN COAST (cont'd)

Campground	Town	Zip	Phone	Water & Electric	Sewer	Pumping/Dump	Store	Laundry	Rec. Hall	Swimming	Boating	Fishing	Pets Allowed	No. of Sites	Season Dates	Map Key
Highland Lake Park	Westbrook	04092	892-8911	X	X	X	N	X	X		X	X	X	50	MD-10/01	C-2
Homestead Campground	Biddeford	04005	282-3239	X	X	X	X	X	X	X	X	X		45	MD-LD	B-2
Indian Rivers Campground	Eliot	03903	748-0844	X	X	X	N	X	X	X	X	X	X	31	5/01-11/01	A-1
King's Pines	Wells	04054	646-4586	X	X	X	X	X	X	X	N	N	X	250	5/15-10/10	A-1
Libby's Ocean-side Camp	York Harbor	03911	363-4171	X	X	X	X	N		X	N	N	X	95	5/15-10/15	A-1
N'er Beach Tent & Trailer Pk	Old Orchard Bch	04064	934-9827	X	X	X	X	X	X	N	N	N	X	58	6/15-LD	B-2
Ocean Overlook	Wells	04090	646-3075	X	X	X	N	N		X	N	N		50	5/15-10/15	B-2
Old Orchard Beach Camping	Old Orchard Bch	04064	934-4477	X	X	X	N	X	X	X	N	N	X	600	4/30-10/01	B-2
Pinderosa Camping Area	Wells	04090	646-2492	X	X	X	X	X				X	X	100	5/15-10/15	B-2
Recompence Shore Camp-sites	Freeport	04032	865-4911	X		X	N	N		X		X	X	90	5/27-9/30	C-3

Name	Town	ZIP	Phone											Sites	Season	Grid
Red Barn Farm Campground	Biddeford	04005	284-4282	X	X	X	X					X	X	60	5/01-10/1	B-2
Riverside Campground	Wells	04090	646-3145	X	X	X	X			X	X	N	X	130	5/15-10/15	B-2
Sea-Vu Campground	Wells	04090	646-7732	X	X	X	X	X	X	N	N	N	X	220	5/10-10/10	B-2
Spruce Lodge Tent & Trailer Pk	Old Orchard Bch	04064	934-2283	X		X	N	N		N			X	184	5/30-9/15	B-2
Stadig Campground	Wells	04090	646-2298	X	X	X	X	X	X					150	5/28-10/1	B-2
Ten Acres Cabins & Campground	Arundel	04046	985-4578	X	N	X	N	N	N	N	N	N	X	40	5/28-LD	B-2
Twin Brooks Camping Area	Gray	04039	428-3832	X			X			X	X	X	X	25	MD-9/15	C-2
Wassamki Springs	Westbrook	04092	839-4276	X	X	X	X	X	X	X	X	X	X	100	5/01-10/15	B-2
Wells Beach Resort	Wells	04090	646-7570	X	X	X	N	X	X	N	N	X	X	175	5/15-CD	B-2
Willey's Hide-A-Way Campground	Saco	04072	282-0502	X	X	X	X	N	X	N	X	X	X	100	5/15-10/1	B-2
Ye Olde Red Barn	York	03909	363-5092	X		X	N	N		X			X	88	5/15-9/10	A-1
Yogi Bear's Jellystone Park	Sanford-Wells	04073	324-7782	X	X	X	X			X	X	X	X	150	5/15-9/15	B-1

2—WESTERN LAKES

Campground	Town	Zip	Phone	Water & Electric	Sewer	Pumping/Dump	Store	Laundry	Rec. Hall	Swimming	Boating	Fishing	Pets Allowed	No. of Sites	Season Dates	Map Key
Acres of Wildlife	Steep Falls	04085	675-3211	X	X	X	X	X	X	X	X	X	X	100	All-Year	C-1
Bay of Naples Family Camping	Naples	04055	693-6429	X	X	X	X	X	X	X	X	X	X	125	5/20-10/16	C-1
Bear Mountain Village	Harrison	04040	583-2541	X		X	X	X	X	X	X	X	X	70	5/15-10/15	D-1
Brookside Grove Campground	South Lebanon	04027	339-9602	X		X	N	X	X		X	X	X	75	5/01-10/01	B-1
Bunganut Lake Camping Area	Alfred	04002	247-3875	X		X	X	X	X	X	X	X	X	110	5/01-10/15	B-1
Canal Bridge Camping Area	Fryeburg	04037	935-2286	X		X	X	X		X	X	X	X	40	5/1-10/15	C-1
Colonial Mast	Naples	04055	693-6652	X	X	X	X	X	X	X	X	X	X	75	MD-CD	C-1
Cupsuptic Campground	Adamstown	04964	864-5249	X	X	X	X	X	X	X	X	X	X	55	5/20-10/1	F-1
Family Circle Campground	Naples	04024	693-6881	X			X	X		X	X	X	X	125	5/15-10/01	C-1
Four Seasons Camping Area	Naples	04055	693-6797	X		X	X	X	X	X	X	X	X	126	5/14-10/11	C-1

Name	Town	Code	Phone	Features									Sites	Season	Grid
Indian Point Camping Area	Raymond	04071	655-4647	X	X	X	X	N	X	X	X		86	5/15-10/1	C-2
Keoka Beach Camping Area	South Waterford	04081	583-2868	X	X		X	X	X	X	X	X	120	5/14-9/25	D-1
Kezar Lake Camping Area	Lovell	04051	925-1631	X		X	X	X	X	X	X		72	5/1-10/15	D-1
King's-Queen's Court Resort	South Lebanon	04027	339-9465	X	X	X	X		X	X			450	5/13-10/02	B-1
Kokatosi Rt. 85 Campground	Raymond	04071	627-4642	X	X	X	X	X	X	X	X	X	150	5/15-9/18	C-2
Lakeside Pines Campground	Bridgton	04057	647-3935	X		X	X	X	X	X	X	X	185	MD-9/15	C-1
Littlefield Beaches	Locke Mills	04219	875-3290	X	X	X		X	X	X	X	X	140	5/15-10/01	D-1
Locklin Camping Area	South Hiram	04047	625-8622	X		N	X		X	X	X	X	45	5/30-LD	C-1
Long Lake Campsites	North Bridgton	04057	647-2321	X		X	X	X	X	X	X	X	160	5/15-9/25	D-1
Muskegon Camping Area	Oxford	04270	539-9689	X		X	X		X	X	X	X	95	5/15-9/15	D-2
Natural High Camping Area	Lebanon	04027	339-9630	X	X	X	X		X	X			187	4/29-CD	B-1
Nokomis Camping Area	Harrison	04040	583-4411	X		X		X	X	X	X	X	30	5/15-9/15	C-1
Papoose Pond Resort & Campground	North Waterford	04267	583-4470	X	X	X	X	X	X	X	X	X	180	5/15-10/15	D-1

2—WESTERN LAKES (cont'd)

Campground	Town	Zip	Phone	Water & Electric	Sewer	Pumping/Dump	Store	Laundry	Rec. Hall	Swimming	Boating	Fishing	Pets Allowed	No. of Sites	Season Dates	Map Key
Point Sebago Out-door Resort	Casco	04015	655-3821	X	X	X	X	X	X	X	X	X	X	496	4/30-10/24	C-2
Salmon Point Campground	Bridgton	04009	647-3678	X	X	X	X	N	X	X	X	X	X	100	5/27-10/16	C-1
Scott's Cove Camping	Alfred	04002	324-6594	X		X	X	N	X	X	X	X	X	50	5/13-9/30	B-1
Sebago Basin Camping Area	North Windham	04062	892-4839	X	X	X	X	X	X	X	X	X	X	170	5/15-10/15	C-2
Simpson's Se-bago Lake Campground	Sebago Lake	04075	787-3671	X	X	X	X	X	X	X	X	X	X	61	5/1-10/1	C-1
South Arm Camp-ground	South Arm	04216	784-3566	X		X			X	X	X	X	X	90	MD-9/15	E-1
Vacationland Campsites	Harrison	04040	583-4953	X		X	X		X	X	X	X	X	125	All-Year	D-1
Vicki-Lin Camping Area	Bridgton	04009	647-2630	X		X	X	X	X	X	X	X	X	90	5/15-10/15	C-1
Walnut Grove Campground	Alfred	04002	324-3448	X	X	X	X	X	X	X	X		X	93	4/1-12/1	B-1

Campground	Town	Zip	Phone	Water & Electric	Sewer	Pumping/Dump	Store	Laundry	Rec. Hall	Swimming	Boating	Fishing	Pets Allowed	No. of Sites	Season Dates	Map Key
Wilderness Campground	Norway	04268	743-2721	X		X	X	X	X	X	X	X	X	50	5/25-10/15	D-1
Woodland Acres	Brownfield	04010	935-2529	X		X	X	X	X	X	X	X	X	50	5/15-10/15	C-1

3—CENTRAL LAKES

Campground	Town	Zip	Phone	Water & Electric	Sewer	Pumping/Dump	Store	Laundry	Rec. Hall	Swimming	Boating	Fishing	Pets Allowed	No. of Sites	Season Dates	Map Key
Allen Pond Campground	Greene	04236	946-7439	X		X	X	X	X		X	X	X	50	5/15-10/15	D-3
Augusta West Lakeside Resort	Winthrop	04364	377-9993	X		X	X	X	X	X	X	X	X	80	5/15-10/30	D-3
Bartlett Campground	Belgrade Lakes	04918	495-3825	X		X	X	X		X	X	X	X	50	5/01-9/30	E-3
Beaver Brook Camping Area	N. Monmouth	04265	933-2108	X		X	X	X	X	X	X	X	X	180	5/1-9/15	D-3
Birches	Litchfield	04350	268-4330	X	X	X	X	X	X	X	X	X	X	109	5/18-9/17	D-3
Gardiner/Richmond KOA	Gardiner/Richmond	04345	582-5086	X	X	X	X	X	X	X	X	X	X	76	5/15-10/15	D-3
Green Valley Campground	Vassalboro	04989	923-3000	X		X	X	X	X	X	X	X	X	70	5/15-9/15	D-4

3—CENTRAL LAKES (cont'd)

Campground	Town	Zip	Phone	Water & Electric	Sewer	Pumping/Dump	Store	Laundry	Rec. Hall	Swimming	Boating	Fishing	Pets Allowed	No. of Sites	Season Dates	Map Key
Martin Stream Campsites	Turner	04282	225-3274	X		X	X			X	X	X	X	30	5/15-10/01	D-2
Range Pond Campground	Poland	04273	998-2624	X	X	X	X	N		X	X	X	X	40	MD-9/6	C-2
Riverbend	Leeds	04263	524-5711	X		X	X	N	X	X	N	X	X	80	5/01-9/15	D-3
Sunset View Tent & Trailer Pk	South China	04358	445-2311	X	X	X	X	X	X	X	X	X	X	100	5/22-9/25	D-4
Teddy Bear Camping Area	North Turner	04266	224-8275	N	N	N	N	N	X	X	X	X	X	20	5/28-9/01	D-2
Timber Trail Campground	Winthrop	04364	395-4376	X		X	X	N	X	X	X	N	X	60	MD-LD	D-3
Vagabond Village	Gardiner	04345	582-1150	X	X	X	X	N	X	X	N	N	X	50	5/15-9/30	D-3

X = available at campground
N = available within 1 mile of campground
E = Electricity only
D = Dryers only

MD = Memorial Day weekend
LD = Labor Day
CD = Columbus Day

4—MID COASTAL

Campground	Town	Zip	Phone	Water & Electric	Sewer	Pumping/Dump	Store	Laundry	Rec. Hall	Swimming	Boating	Fishing	Pets Allowed	No. of Sites	Season Dates	Map Key
Atticus Hill Farm Camping Area	Thomaston	04861	354-6266	X						X			X	65	5/15-9/30	C-5
Camden Campground	Camden	04843	236-2478	X		X	X	X		X	X	X	X	84	MD-LD	D-5
Camp Sequin	Georgetown	04548	371-2777				X		X	N	N	X	X	30	5/15-9/15	C-4
Chewonki Campgrounds	Wiscasset	04578	882-7426	X		X	X		X	X	X	X	X	47	5/15-10/15	C-4
Duck Puddle Campground	Nobleboro	04555	563-5608	X		X	X			X	X	X	X	80	5/15-9/15	D-4
Hermit Island	Small Point	04567	443-2101	X	X	X	X	D	X	X	X	X	X	273	5/15-10/15	C-3
Lake Pemaquid Camping	Damariscotta	04543	563-5202	X	X	X	X	X	X	X	X	X	X	200	5/01-9/30	C-4
Little Ponderosa Campground	Boothbay	04537	633-2700	X		X	X	X	X	X	X	X	X	90	5/15-10/15	C-4
Meadowbrook Camping Area	Bath	04530	443-4967	X		X	X	X	X			X	X	100	All-Year	C-3
Megunticook by the Sea	Rockport	04856	594-2428	X		X	X	X		X	X	X	X	100	5/15-10/15	D-5

4—MID COASTAL (cont'd)

Campground	Town	Zip	Phone	Water & Electric	Sewer	Pumping/Dump	Store	Laundry	Rec. Hall	Swimming	Boating	Fishing	Pets Allowed	No. of Sites	Season Dates	Map Key
Mic Mac Cove	Union	04862	785-4100	X	X	X	X	N	X	X	X	X	X	85	5/15-9/15	D-5
Northport Travel Park	Belfast	04915	338-2077	X	X	X	X	X	X	X		X	X	62	5/1-10/15	D-5
Ocean View Park	Popham Beach	04562	389-2564	X	X	X	N			X	N	X	X	47	5/20-9/19	C-3
Orr's Island Campground	Orr's Island	04066	833-5595	X	X	X	X			X	X	X	X	50	MD-9/15	C-3
Searsport Shores Campground	Searsport	04915	548-6059	X		X	X	N	X	X	X	X	X	139	4/15-11/1	D-5
Sherwood Forest Campsite	Pemaquid Beach	04554	677-3642	X		X	X	X	X	N	N	X	N	80	5/15-10/15	C-4
Shore Hills Campground	Boothbay	04537	633-4782	X		X	X	X	X	N	N	X	X	100	5/10-9/27	C-4
Thomas Point Beach	Brunswick	04011	725-6009				N	N	X	X		X	X	25	5/30-9/1	C-3
Town Line Campsites	Nobleboro	04572	832-7055	X	X	X	X	X	X	X	X	X	X	55	5/27-LD	C-2
West Sennebec Campsites	Appleton	04862	785-4250	X	X	X	X	X	X	X	X	X	X	75	MD-9/15	D-5

5—NORTHERN LAKES & FORESTS

Campground	Town	Zip	Phone	Water & Electric	Sewer	Pumping/Dump	Store	Laundry	Rec. Hall	Swimming	Boating	Fishing	Pets Allowed	No. of Sites	Season Dates	Map Key
Abanaki Camping Center	Madison	04976	474-2070	X		X	X	X	X	X	X	X	X	103	5/15-10/15	E-3
Abol Bridge Campground	Millinocket	04462					X			X		X	X	37	5/15-9/30	H-5
Allagash Gateway Campsite	Greenville	04441	676-2715	X			X			X	X	X	X	30	5/15-11/30	H-5
Allagash Wilderness Outfitters	Greenville	04441	695-2821							X	X	X	X	10	5/15-9/30	G-4
Happy Horseshoe Campground	N. New Portland	04961	628-3471	X		X	X	X	X	X	N	X	X	50	MD-9/24	E-3
Jo-Mary Lake Campground	E. Millinocket	04430					X	X	X	X	X	X	X	50	5/15-SNOW	G-5
Katahdin Area Camping	Medway	04460	746-9349	X	X	X	X	X	X	X	X	X	X	108	4/15-12/1	G-6
Matagamon Wilderness Cpgrnd	Patten	04765					X			X	X	X	X	36	5/01-12/01	H-6
Moose River Campground	Jackman	04945	668-3341	X		X	X	X	X	X	X	X	X	42	5/15-10/15	G-2

5—NORTHERN LAKES & FORESTS (cont'd)

Campground	Town	Zip	Phone	Water & Electric	Sewer	Pumping/Dump	Store	Laundry	Rec. Hall	Swimming	Boating	Fishing	Pets Allowed	No. of Sites	Season Dates	Map Key
Natanis Point	Eustis	04936	297-2601	X		X				X	X	X	X	60	MD-LD	F-2
Nor' 40 Campground	Farmington	04938	778-3275	X	N	X		X	X	X	N	X	X	50	5/15-10/15	E-2
Northern Whitewater Camps/Campground	The Forks	04985	663-2271	X							X	X		20	5/20-9/30	G-3
Old Mill Campground & Cabins	Rockwood	04478	534-7333	X		X	X	X	X	X	X	X	X	50	All-Year	G-4
Pine Grove Campground	E. Millinocket	04430	746-5172	X		X	X	X	X	X	X	X	X	30	5/20-10/15	G-6
Shin Pond Village	Patten	04765	528-2900	X		X	X	X	X	X	N	X	X	20	5/01-11/30	H-6
Somerset Campground	Norridgewock	04957	634-4952	X	X	X	N	N		X	N	N	X	44	5/1-12/1	E-3
Tent Village Campground	Newport	04953	368-5047	X		X	X	X	X	X	X	X	X	40	5/15-10/15	E-5
Togue Pond Camps & Campground	Millinocket	04462					X			X	X	X	X	31	5/1-12/1	H-6

6—PENOBSCOT / ACADIA

Campground	Town	Zip	Phone	Water & Electric	Sewer	Pumping/Dump	Store	Laundry	Rec. Hall	Swimming	Boating	Fishing	Pets Allowed	No. of Sites	Season Dates	Map Key
Balsam Cove Campground	East Orland	04431	469-7771	X		X	N	X	X	X	X	X	X	60	5/26-10/15	E-6
Barcadia Tent & Trailer Ground	Bar Harbor	04609	288-3520	X	X	X	X	X	X	X	X	X	X	200	5/25-10/03	D-7
Bass Harbor Campground	Bass Harbor	04653	244-5857	X	X	X	X	X	X	N	N	N	X	130	5/23-10/1	D-7
Branch Lake Camping Area	Ellsworth	04605	667-5174	X	X	X	X	X	X	X	X	X	X	50	4/01-12/01	E-7
Frenchman's Bay Resort Campground	Bar Harbor	04605	667-4300	X	X	X	X	X	X	X			X	140	5/25-10/15	D-7
Gatherings	Ellsworth	04605	667-8826	X	X	X	X	X	X	X	X	X	X	100	5/01-10/15	E-7
Hadley's Point Campground	Bar Harbor	04609	288-4808	X	X	X	X	X		X	N	N	X	180	5/15-10/15	B-7
Hammond Street Camping	Bangor	04401	848-3455	X	X	X	X			X			X	200	5/15-10/20	E-6
Lakeside Camping	Enfield	04433	732-4241	X	X	X	X	X	X	X	X	X	X	34	5/1-10/31	F-6

6—PENOBSCOT / ACADIA

Campground	Town	Zip	Phone	Water & Electric	Sewer	Pumping/Dump	Store	Laundry	Rec. Hall	Swimming	Boating	Fishing	Pets Allowed	No. of Sites	Season Dates	Map Key
Mainayr Campground	Steuben	04680	546-2690	X	X	X	X	X		X	X	X	X	35	MD-10/15	E-8
Masthead Campground	Bucksport	04416	469-3482	X	X	X	X	X		X	X	X	X	45	MD-CD	E-6
Mountainview Campground	East Sullivan	04607	422-6215	X	X	X	X			X	X	X	X	50	MD-10/01	E-7
Mt. Desert Campground	Mount Desert	04660	244-3710	X			N			X	X	X	X	200	5/15-10/01	D-7
Mt. Desert Narrows	Bar Harbor	04609	288-4782	X	X	X	X	X	X	X	X	X	X	300	5/15-10/15	D-7
Parks Pond Campground	Clifton	04428	843-7360	X	X	X	X	X	X	X	X	X	X	75	MD-LD	E-6
Patten Pond KOA	Ellsworth	04605	667-5745	X	X	X	X	X	X	X	X	X	X	158	5/1-11/1	E-6
Pleasant Hill Campground	Bangor	04401	848-5127	X	X	X	X	X	X	X	X	X	X	105	5/01-10/20	E-6
Pleasant Lake Shores	Stetson	04488	296-2041	X			X	X		N	N	X	X	35	5/28-9/6	E-5
Smuggler's Den	Southwest Hrbr	04679	244-3944	X	X	X	X	X	X	N	N	N	X	100	5/26-9/15	D-7

Name	Town	ZIP	Phone												Sites	Season	Map
Somes Sound View	Mt. Desert	04660	244-5452	X						X	N	X	X	X	70	MD-10/7	D-7
Whispering Pines	East Orland	04431	469-3443	X	X	X	N		X	X	X	X	X	45	5/20-9/10	E-6
White Birches	Southwest Hrbr	04679	244-3797	X	X	X	N		X	N	N	X	X	60	5/15-10/15	D-7

7—WASHINGTON COUNTY

Name	Town	ZIP	Phone												Sites	Season	Map
Greenland Cove Campground	Danforth	04424	448-2863	X		X		X	X	X	X	X	X	50	5/10-9/30	G-8
Keenes Lake Camping Ground	Red Beach	04670	454-7411	X		X		X	X	X	X	X	X	115	5/15-10/01	F-10
Seaview	Eastport	04631	853-4471	X	X	X	X	N	X	X	X	X	X	40	5/15-10/15	F-10
Sunrise Shores	Perry	04667	853-6608	X	X	X	X	X	X	X	B	B	X	170	5/15-9/30	F-10
Sunset Point Trailer Park	Lubec	04652	733-2150	X	N	X	X	X	X	N	X	X	X	40	5/15-10/15	E-10

8—AROOSTOOK COUNTY

Name	Town	ZIP	Phone												Sites	Season	Map
Birch Point Log Lodge and Campground	Island Falls	04747	463-2515	X	X	X	X	X	X	X	X	X	X	75	5/1-11/1	H-7
My Brother's Place	Houlton	04730	532-6739	X	X	X	X	X	X	X	X	X	X	100	5/15-10/15	I-8
Neil E. Michaud Campground	Presque Isle	04769	768-7751	X		X			X					45	5/01-10/15	J-8
Uncle Noel's	Caribou	04736	498-2491	X					X					10	6/1-9/30	J-8

■ Wilderness Lodging

32 Sporting Camps

The lodges and cabins listed below all provide excellent brochures, often in color, which explain rates, reservations, and answer most questions you might think to ask. Their seasons vary slightly but are usually open "ice out to Sept." Some are year round. This list includes those catering to fishermen, hunters, and "relaxers."

Map	Name
G-8	**Anderson's East Grand Camps** Box 97, Greenland Avenue, Danforth, ME 04424, Tel. (207) 448–2455. Modern conveniences, boats, motors, and guides. Season is year round.
F-1	**Bosebuck Mountain Camps** Wilson Mills, ME 04293. Tel. (207) 243–2945. Winter address: P.O. Box 106, Kearsarge, NH 03847, Tel. (603) 356–6433. A unique wilderness fishing experience in tradition of original sporting camps.
G-2,3	**Bull Dog Camps** Enchanted Lake, West Forks, ME 04985, Tel. (207) 243–2853. Winter address: RFD #2, Box 2475, Brunswick, ME Tel. (207)725–4742. Beautiful secluded lake, only camps there. Access is by hiking, float plane, or 4-WD over jeep trail (Mid-May to Sept. 30).
H-4	**Chesuncook Village** Rte. 76, Box 655, Greenville, ME 04441. Built in 1864, center of historic logging industry, near mouth of Penobscot River, on NW shore Chesuncook Lake.
F-8	**Chet's Camps on Big Lake** P.O. Princeton, ME 04668. Center of fishing tradition, near Grand Lake Stream.
G-2	**Cozy Cove Cabins** SR64, Box 45, Jackman, ME 04945, Tel. (207) 668–5931. Modern housekeeping cabins on scenic Big Wood Lake. Season is year round.

Map	Name
F-1	**The Farm House** P.O. Box 173, Rangeley, ME 04970, Tel. (207) 864-3446. Country suites, bunk-houses, nice people to know. You'll like your stay.
EF-1	**Flybuck Camps** Box 222A, Oquossoc, ME 04964, Tel. (207) 864-5574. On Rangeley Lake, 1–4 bedroom cottages, sandy beach.
GH-5	**Frost Pond Camps** Winter: 36 Minuteman Drive, Millinocket, ME, Tel. (207) 723-6622. Summer: Box 620, Star Rt. 76, Greenville, ME, Radio contact (207) 695-2821. Rustic cabins in heart of Maine woods, fishing, boating, canoeing. Open May 1–Nov. 30.
G-2	**Grace Pond Camps** P.O. Box 149, Jackman, ME 04945, Tel. (207) 243-2949. Nature, brook trout, log cabins. Season May 15th through hunting season.
G-4	**Hardscrabble Lodge** Box 360, Greenville Junction, ME 04442, Tel. (207) 695-2881. Originally headquarters for huge lumber crews in late 1800's. Lodges are hand-crafted, notched spruce logs. Ice out, mid-May. (Usually!) Best access is 20 minute float plane hop with Folsom's Air Service from Greenville.
GH-4	**Lobster Lake Camps** Lobster Lake Camps, Rockwood, ME 04478. Winter address: P.O. Box 103, Center Tuftonboro, NH 03816, Tel. (603) 569-1219. Rustic wood-heated camps on beautiful, wild, Maine lake. Housekeeping only. Season ice out (May 1 ±) to Thanksgiving.
F-1	**The Mooselookmegunticook House** Modern housekeeping cottages on the lake, fireplaces, marina. Haines Marina Landing, Rangeley, ME 04970, Tel. (207) 864-3627.
H-6	**Mt. Chase Lodge** Upper Shin Pond, Patten, ME 04765, Tel. (207) 528-2183. Baxter State Park within easy drive, open all year, special packages.
G-4	**Mt. Kineo Cabins** P.O. Box 115 MS, Rockwood, ME 04478, Tel. (207) 534-7744. Eight waterfront cabins, boats, canoes, moose watching, view of Mt. Kineo.
F-1	**Mt. View Cottages** Box 284, Oquossoc, ME 04964, Tel. (207) 864-3416. 5 Rustic housekeeping cottages spaced for privacy along 800′ of lake frontage. Boat, motor, canoe, sailboat rentals.

Map	Name

G-5   **Nahmakanta Lake Wilderness Log Cabins**   Box 85-W, Andover, ME 04216, Tel. (207) 392-2222. Remote, located on beautiful 4 mile lake. Access to other ponds. $1.00 for color brochure.

F-7   **Nicatous Lodge & Camps**   Burlington, ME 04417. Remote and relaxing. Secluded cabins and lodges on 12 mile Nicatous Lake. Open 4 seasons.

F-1   **North Camps**   Rangeley, ME 04970, Tel. (207) 864-2247. 12 Housekeeping cottages on Rangeley Lake, beach, boats, canoe, sailboat rentals.

FG-3   **Northern Outdoor Lodge**   The Forks, ME 04985. Tel. (207) 663-2249. Modern facility, yet offers remote deer hunts, fishing, rafting, or just plain relaxing. Open year round.

H-2   **Penobscot Lake Lodge**   P.O. Box 1149, Greenville, ME 04441. Lodge can be reached by road and short boat ride. Best, however, is a beautiful flight from Greenville. Beautiful unspoiled lake.

H-4   **Camp Phoenix on Nesowadnehunk Lake**   T5R10, Box 210, Millinocket, ME 04462, Tel. (207) 695-2821. (No. is Folsom's Flying Service radio contact with Lodge.) Trout, mountain hikes, Baxter Park.

F-1   **Pleasant Island Lodge & Cottages**   Oquossoc, ME 04964, Tel. (207) 864-3722. 13 housekeeping log cabins on Cupsuptic Lake, fireplaces, boats, motors.

F-9   **Pocomoonshine Lodges**   Alexander, ME 04694, Tel. (207) 454-2310. Comfortable housekeeping cottages, fishing bases, boats, and swimming.

GH-5   **Pray's Housekeeping Cottages**   Star Route, Box 605, Greenville, ME 04441, Tel. (207) 723-8880. Salmon pool, excellent area for all outdoor activities, including rafting.

EF-2   **Quimby Pond Camps**   Rangeley, ME 04970, Tel. (207) 864-3675. Rustic housekeeping cottages, automatic heat. Famous 165 acre trout pond challenges you in the land that made fishing history.

G-2   **Red Buck Camps**   P.O. Box 114, Jackman, ME 04945, Tel. (207) 668-5361. Modern log cabins on Parlin Pond, 4 seasons.

Map	Name

G-4   **Rockwood Cottages** Box 176S, Rockwood, ME 04478. Housekeeping cottages on shore of Moosehead, view of Mt. Kineo.

EF-2   **Russell's Motor Camps** Box 106B, Rangeley, ME 04970, Tel. (207) 864-2204. Housekeeping and overnight cottages on shore of lake.

EF-2   **Saddleback Lake Lodge** Box 620, Rangeley, ME 04970, Tel. (207) 864-5501. Swimming, fishing, canoeing, sandy beach.

G-2   **Sally Mt. Cabins** SR 64, Box 50, Sally Mt. Cabins, Jackman, ME 04945, Tel. (207) 668-5621. Log cabins on shore of Big Wood Lake in heart of what is sometimes called the "Switzerland of Maine." Canada 18 miles away.

EF-4   **Sandy Bay Camps** Greenville, ME 04441, Tel. (207) 695-2512. 4 seasons, furnished camps, sandy beach, white water canoeing.

EF-2   **Sequoia** Rt. #17, Oquossoc, ME 04964, Tel. (207) 864-3492. Housekeeping cabins on Rangeley Lake.

H-6   **Shin Pond Camps** RFD #1, Box 279, Patten, ME 04765, Tel. (207) 528-2963. Near entrance to Baxter State Park, 50 acres overlooking Shin Pond. Open for first time in 7 years, new management.

G-2   **Sky Lodge** Box 99, Moose River, ME 04945, Tel. (207) 668-2171. Private airfield El 1350, RW 1700′, grass. Open year round, "luxury in the rough."

GH-6   **South Branch Lake Camps** Sebois, ME 04484. A sportsman's home in the tall pines. Boats and canoes.

G-4   **Spencer Pond Camps** Star Route 76, Box 580, Greenville, ME 04441. Located in heart of Moosehead region and foothills of Little Spencer Mt. Complete list of activities available.

F-2   **Sugarloaf Inn Resort** On the mountain, Carrabassett Valley, ME 04947, Tel. 1-800-343-4075. Lots of outdoor packages. Is remote, yet is a resort, not true wilderness lodge.

G-3,4   **Sundown Cabins** Box 117, Rockwood, ME 04478, Tel. (207) 534-7357. Housekeeping cabins on Moosehead, excellent view of Mt. Kineo. Year round.

Map	Name
F-1	**Sundown Cottages** Box 40, Oquossoc, ME 04964, Tel. (207) 864-3650. Swimming, sailing, fishing, cycling. Quiet setting.
F-1	**The Swiss Colony** Box 597, Rangeley, ME 04970, Tel. (207) 864-3760. 4 seasons resort nestled in mountain's east shore of Rangeley Lake.
F-2	**Tea Pond Camps** P.O. Box 349, Stratton, ME 04982, Tel. (207) 243-2943 or 246-6371. Rustic log cabins, home cooked food, special camping and canoe trips available.
F-2	**Tim Pond Wilderness Camps** Box 22, Eustis, ME 04936, Tel. (207) 243-2947. 1000 acres of scenic splendor. Native brook trout only, hunting, canoeing available.
G-3	**Tomhegan Wilderness Lodges** Box 8, Rockwood, ME 04478. Access by car from Rockwood on good gravel road. Log cabins, open all year, unique boardwalk connects all facilities.
G-3,4	**Wilson's on Moosehead** Greenville Jct., ME 04472, Tel. (207) 695-2549. Located at headwaters of Kennebec River on west shore of Moosehead Lake.
FG-3	**Woody's** on Moose River at Moosehead Lake Rockwood, ME 04478, Tel. (207) 534-7752. Fishing, boating, canoes.

Some less remote accommodations located in very desirable vacation settings

Map	Name
G-4	**Camp Allagash** Greenville, ME 04441, Tel. (207) 695-2532. Located Bolton Cove, Moosehead Lake. Housekeeping cottages, campsites, RV hookups.
EF-2	**Bald Mt. Camps** Oquossoc, ME 04964, Tel. (207) 864-3671. American Plan for fishing and vacation.
G-4	**Beaver Cove Camps** Box 1233-M, Greenville, ME 04441, Tel. (207) 695-3717. Housekeeping cabins on Moosehead Lake.
G-3,4	**The Birches** Rockwood, ME 04478, Tel. (207) 534-7305. You'll get to enjoy your stay here. 17 hand hewn cabins in grove of birches. Full season, fishing, canoeing, local or remote. Everyone knows "The Birches."

Map	Name
G-4	**Chalet Moosehead** On shore of Moosehead. Birch Street, Box 327-M, Greenville Jct., ME 04442.
D-3	**Echo Lake Lodge & Cottages** Winter: P.O. Box 1186, Katy, Texas 77449, Tel. (713) 574-4584. Summer: P.O. Box 206, Kents Hill, ME 04349, Tel. (207) 685-3593. Located west of Augusta, clean lake, good fishing.
G-4	**Gray Ghost Camps** Box 35, Rockwood, ME 04478, Tel. (207) 534-7362. Housekeeping cottages on Moose River. Open all year.
G-4	**Greenwood Motel** Greenville Jct., 04442, Tel. (207) 695-3321. Motel setting but in heart of wilderness and ski area.
F-4	**Hartley's** RFD #1, Box 48R, Dover-Foxcroft, ME 04426, Tel. (207) 564-2009. New cottages on 15 mile Sebec Lake. Privacy a key, some sites are remote.
G-2	**Hillcrest Motel & Restaurant** Jackman, ME 04945, Tel. (207) 668-2721. Back country fly fishing, golf, canoeing, tennis.
G-4	**Indian Hill Motel** Greenville, ME 04441. Tel. (207) 695-2623. Called gateway to Moosehead region. Panoramic view of Moosehead.
EF-4	**Leisure Life Lodge** Greenville, ME 04441, Tel. (207) 695-3737. New lodge near "downtown" Greenville. Restaurant, bar, pool.

33 Hunting Camps

The following hunting lodges and camps have provided both Maine residents and non-residents with hours of fun, excitement, and relaxation. Each has a clear brochure that fully describes its facilities and services.

Map Key	Name and Address	Ducks	Deer	Woodcock & Grouse	Bear	Bobcat	Coyote	Moose
H-7	**Bear Creek Guide Service** Box 367 Island Falls, ME 04747, Tel. (207) 463-2662		x		x		x	
H-7	**Bear Mountain Lodge** Smyrna Mills, ME 04780, Tel. (207) 528-2124		x	x	x		x	
G-4	**Beaver Cove Camps** Box 1233-M, Greenville, ME 04441, Tel. (207) 695-3717	x	x	x				x
J-6	**Big Machias Lake Camps** Ashland, ME, 04732, Tel. (207) 435-6977		x		x			
H-7	**Camp Wapiti** Patten, ME 04765, Tel. (207) 528-2485		x		x			x
G-4	**Chalet Moosehead** Birch St., Box 327-M Greenville Jct., ME 04442 Tel. (207) 695-2950		x	x	x			x
F-9	**Chet's Camps on Big Lake** P.O. Princeton, ME 04668, Tel. (Winter) (207) 427-3826, (Camp) (207) 796-5557			x				
E-5	**Coastal Maine Outfitters, Inc.** RFD #1, Box 2380, Brooks, ME 04921, Tel. (207) 722-3218	x	x					
G-2	**Cozy Cove Cabins** Jackman Station, ME 04945 Tel. (207) 668-5931				x			x
G-3	**Crabapple Acres Inn** The Forks, ME 04985, Tel. (207) 663-2218		x	x	x			

Map Key	Name and Address	Ducks	Deer	Woodcock & Grouse	Bear	Bobcat	Coyote	Moose
G-7	**Deer Run Sporting Camps** P.O. Kingman, ME 04451, Tel. (Summer) (207) 765-3900		x		x			
G-4	**First Roach Lodge** Star Route 76, Box 588, Greenville, ME 04441, Tel. (207) 695-2890		x	x	x			x
F-1	**Flybuck Camps** Box 222A, Oquossoc, ME 04964, Tel. (207) 864-5575		x	x				
H-5	**Frost Pond Camps** Box 620, Star Route 76, Greenville, ME 04441, Radio contact: (207) 695-2821		x					
B-2	**Gardner's Hunting Lodge** RFD #5, Cape Elizabeth, ME 04104, Tel. (207) 799-2341, (Hunting Frye Mt)		x	x			x	
G-4	**Gentle Ben's Hunting Lodge** Box 212, Rockwood, ME 04478, Tel. (207) 534-2201		x		x	x		
G-2	**Grace Pond Camps** P.O. Box 149, Jackman, ME 04945, Tel. (207) 243-2949		x		x			
G-4	**Hardscrabble Lodge** Box 360, Greenville Jct., ME 04442 Tel. (207) 695-2881		x					
G-2	**Hillcrest Motel & Restaurant** Jackman, ME 04945, Tel. (207) 668-2721			x				

Map Key	Name and Address	Ducks	Deer	Woodcock & Grouse	Bear	Bobcat	Coyote	Moose
H-7	**Katahdin Lodge & Camp** RFD #1, Box 41-HM, Smyrna Mills, ME 04780, Tel. (207) 528-2131		x		x		x	x
G-2	**Last Resort Lodge & Cabins** Long Lake, Box 1412 ATH Jackman, ME 04945, Tel. (207) 668-5091		x		x			
E-6	**Lazy Loon Guide Service** Brewer, ME 04412, Tel. (207) 989-4995							x
G-4	**Lincoln's Camps** P.O. Box 2955, Rockwood, ME 04478	x	x		x		x	
G-4	**Lobster Lake Camps** Rockwood, ME 04478		x					
H-6	**Mt. Chase Lodge** Upper Shin Pond, Patten, ME 04765		x					
G-4	**Mt. Kineo Cabins** P.O. Box 115 MS, Rockwood, ME 04478, Tel. (207) 534-7744		x	x	x			
F-7	**Nicatous Lodge & Camps** Burlington, ME 04417		x					
G-3	**North Pines** Rt. 201, West Forks, ME 04985, Tel. (207) 663-2277		x		x			
G-3	**Northern Outdoors** The Forks, ME 04985, Tel. (207) 663-2271		x		x	x		

Map Key	Name and Address	Ducks	Deer	Woodcock & Grouse	Bear	Bobcat	Coyote	Moose
G-2	**NW Maine Outfitters** P.O. Box 306, Jackman, ME 04945, Tel. (207) 668-5931				x			
G-4	**Pray's Housekeeping Cottages** Star Route, Box 605, Greenville, ME 04441, Tel. (207) 723-8880		x					
F-1	**Quimby Pond Camps** Rangeley, ME 04970, Tel. (207) 864-3675		x	x				
G-2	**Red Buck Camps** P.O. Box 114, Jackman, ME 04945, Tel. (207) 668-5361		x	x	x	x		
I-7	**Rivers Bend Camps** Masardis, ME 04759, Tel. (207) 761-4495		x		x			
H-7	**Shin Pond Camps** RFD 1, Box 279, Patten, ME 04765, Tel. (207) 528-2963		x					x
G-6	**South Branch Lake Camps** Sebois, ME 04484		x					
G-4	**Spencer Pond Camps** Star Route 76, Box 580, Greenville, ME 04441		x	x	x			
F-2	**Tea Pond Camps** P.O. Box #18, Eustis, ME 04936, Tel. (207) 243-2943		x	x				
F-2	**Tim Pond Wilderness Camps** Box 22, Eustis, ME 04936, Tel. (207) 897-2100		x		x			

Map Key	Name and Address	Ducks	Deer	Woodcock & Grouse	Bear	Bobcat	Coyote	Moose
G-4	**Tomhegan Wilderness Lodge & Cottages** P.O. Box 8, Rockwood, ME 04478, Tel. (207) 534-7712		x					
K-6	**Track Down Kennel Services** RFD #1, Box 1365, Fort Kent, ME 04743, Tel. (207) 834-3612				x			
G-2	**Wildwood Lakeside Cabins** Forest Street, Jackman, ME 04945, Tel. (207) 668-3351	x	x	x	x		x	x
G-4	**Wilson's on Moosehead Lake** Greenville Junction, ME 04442, Tel. (207) 695-2549		x	x				
G-4	**Woody's** Rockwood, ME 04478, Tel. (207) 534-7752		x	x	x			

■ Hunting

34 Hunting Laws

Some hunting regulations remain standard from year to year.

1. Hunters *16 years of age* or older need a hunting license.
2. *Archery* requires a license.

182

3. *Guides* who are paid for services need a Guide License.

4. *Closed season* means you may not hunt any species of wild animal for which an "open season" has been established.

5. It is unlawful to hunt wild *birds* from sunset until 1/2 hour before sunrise. It is unlawful to hunt wild *animals* from 1/2 hour after sunset until 1/2 hour before sunrise except raccoons. NOTE: during deer season all hunting ends at *sunset,* except raccoons.

6. *Loaded firearms* are not permitted in a motor vehicle unless you hold a valid permit (then only pistol or revolver.)

7. A *muzzle loader* is considered "loaded" when charged with powder, lead, and cap installed.

8. *Lights* may not be used except for raccoon.

9. You may not hunt from a *motor vehicle,* trailer, or motorboat. Paraplegics, single or double amputees of the legs may hunt from stationary vehicles.

10. It is unlawful to hunt on *Sunday* in Maine.

11. It is unlawful to hunt from a *paved way.* "Paved way" means a road with bituminous or concrete surface, including the right-of-way of such road.

12. You may not shoot any domestic animal.

13. It is unlawful to hunt while *under the influence* of liquor or drugs.

14. You may not shoot closer than *100 yards* to a dwelling.

15. *Tree stands* are legal in Maine.

35 Equipment Laws

1. *10 gauge* is the maximum size shotgun that may be used.

2. Migratory birds cannot be hunted unless the gun has been *plugged* so that no more than *three shells* can be inserted.

3. *Crossbows* are illegal in Maine.

4. *All Terrain Vehicles* (ATV's) must be registered to operate in the State of Maine. Application forms may be obtained through Dept. Inland Fisheries and Wildlife, 284 State Street,

Station 41, Augusta, ME 04333, the local warden, or town office. The fee for registration is $5.00 per year.

If your snowmobile or ATV is registered out of state, Maine will generally give reciprocity but there is no formal agreement. Suggest you contact your own State Fish & Wildlife to confirm this.

5. It is illegal to hunt with *fully* automatic firearms.
6. *Hunter fluorescent orange* visible from all sides is required during deer season.

---

36 More Information

Bucks Only Law Maine is attempting to help its deer herd by protecting *does,* so look over the map carefully before hunting, and write to Department of Inland Fisheries and Wildlife, 284 State Street, Station 41, Augusta, ME 04333, to see how these regulations in these zones might change. There is strong talk of *doe* permits by zone as a way to manage the herd, *so watch for this in the near future.*

Moose Lottery Maine allows hunting of moose through a lottery system. Nine hundred resident and one hundred non-resident hunters are chosen by random selection in a state lottery. To obtain entry to the lottery request an application from Inland Fisheries and Wildlife, 284 State Street, Station 41, Augusta, ME 04333. Do this between February and April. Exact hunting dates will be sent to you.

The permit drawing is usually held the first week in June. Each zone (see moose zone map page 186) is allowed a specified number of permits for management purposes.

Hunter Safety Courses New, watch for this. After January 1, 1986 any licensed hunter holding a license for the first time will be required to *pass* an approved *Hunter's Safety Course* of ten hours.

a. If you come from any state that has a mandatory hunter safety course, Maine will accept this.
b. If you have hunted in Maine during the last ten years, you are exempt from hunter safety. *HOWEVER,* you must prove, by having saved your old hunting license, that you actually held one! The state can only verify back for *one year.* So watch this and make your plans accordingly.

   Write to Department of Inland Fisheries & Wildlife for additional data.

Duck Stamp In addition to the Federal duck stamp, a Maine waterfowl stamp is required for all waterfowl hunting. Current price is $2.50 and it may be purchased from *Dept. Inland Fisheries & Wildlife,* your Maine local warden, or town office.

NOTE: For *Trapping Seasons,* request regulations from Department of Inland Fisheries & Wildlife since these are under frequent change.

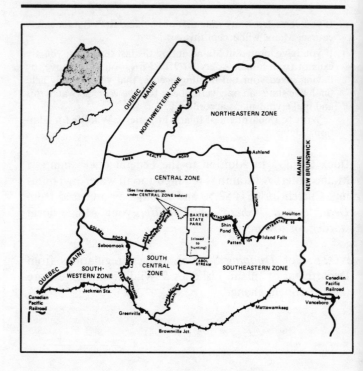

DEER HUNTING ZONE MAP

39 Hunting Safety

Being a safe hunter is mostly a matter of common sense, but there are well-established rules worthy of repeating.

- Treat every gun as if it were loaded at all times, and never point it at a person.
- Whenever a gun is brought into a house, camp, or other building it must be unloaded.
- Check the barrel and action frequently to make sure they are clear.
- Carry your gun at all times so that you can control the direction of the barrel in case of a stumble or fall.
- Be positive of your target before you pull the trigger.
- Never point a gun at anything you don't intend to shoot.
- A gun should be unloaded when left unattended.
- Never climb a tree or a fence, or jump a ditch or other obstacle with a loaded gun.
- Don't fire at a hard flat surface or the surface of water with a gun.
- No intoxicating beverages should be consumed before or during a hunt.

40 Maine Gun Clubs

If you are a gun club member from another state and would like to talk up "bench rests," "NRA," "skeet fields," "trap ranges," etc., then the clubs below will be a good source for you.

Auburn Rifle Club, Inc., Byron G. Ames, 154½ Lake St., Auburn 04210

Auburn Skeet Club, Eugene St. Pierre, 57 Loring Avenue, Auburn 04210.

Bath Rifle and Pistol Assoc., Elmer Fox, 305 Center St., Bath 04530

Big Pine Gun Club, Box 37, Abbot 04406, David E. Armstrong, president.

Blue Hill Rifle and Pistol Club, Clare F. Geindal, P. O. Box 213, Sedgwick 04676.

Bridgton Rifle Club, Inc., RFD #1, Box 152, Denmark 04022.

Capitol City Rifle and Pistol Club, P. O. Box 1025, Augusta 04330, Bert Hayford, president.

Cumberland Rifle and Pistol Club, John N. Fossett, 333 Maine St., Cumberland 04021.

Eye of the Hawk Muzzleloaders, Torpacka's Gun Shop, North Main St., Rockland 04841.

Gould Academy Rifle Club, Box 436, Church St., Bethel 04217.

Hampden Rifle and Pistol Club, Ed L. Baker, RFD #1, Box 7, Hampden Highland 04445.

Hermon Skeet and Trap Club, P. O. Box 1132, Bangor 04401, John Field, president.

Houlton Rifle and Pistol Club, David L. Grant, 37 Franklin St., Houlton 04730.

Island View Skeet Club, Alicia M. Sedgely, RR1, River Road, Bowdoinham 04008.

Maine Muzzle Loading Rifle Assoc., Anna Delaware, Dresser Road, Scarborough 04074.

Maine Skeet Shooting Association, Howell Copp, P. O. Box 501, Gray 04039.

National Muzzle Loading Rifle Assoc., Hugh L. Awalt, 9 Greenwood Court, Augusta 04330.

Pine Tree State Rifle and Pistol Association, P. O. Box 219, Rumford 04276.

Rumford Rifle and Pistol Club, 526 Knox Street, Rumford 04276, Thomas Williams, president.

Scarborough Gun Club, Wayne Morse, 236 Gray Road, Falmouth 04105.

Somerset County Muzzle Loader, Ronald Oliver, Pleasant Street, North Anson 04958.

Southern Maine Small Bore League, John Fossett, 333 Main Street, Cumberland 04021.

This is a list of gun clubs compiled from the latest information available. There are a number of sportsmen's clubs which also have shooting fields which are not listed here. Inquiries should be sent to: The Maine Sportsman, Box 365, Augusta, ME 04330.

■ Skiing

41 Cross-Country

Maine has made serious efforts to become a true four-season area. In this regard numerous inns and resorts have established cross-country ski trails that connect directly to their door. Others are available to the public in state parks.

Acadia National Park
Bar Harbor, ME 04609 (Map Key D-7)
Tel. (207) 288-3338
43 miles of cross-country skiing on carriage roads from which
snowmobiles are mostly excluded. No grooming. Spectacular
mountain and ocean views. Conditions vary due to proximity to
the ocean. Lodging is available in nearby towns.
Directions: Drive to Mt. Desert Island, follow Rt. 3 to Bar Harbor
(do not follow signs for downtown), watch for Rt. 233, turn west
on 233, drive 3 miles to Park H.Q., receive trail map here.

Acadian Ski Touring
Hermon, ME 04401 (Map Key E-6)
No telephone
Five miles of marked and groomed trails. Instruction and rentals.
Directions: Arrive in Bangor, travel northwest out of Bangor on
Rt. 2 or 222 to the Billings Road in Hermon, see signs.

Akers Ski Center
Andover, ME 04216 (Map Key E-1)
Tel. (207) 392-4582
Six miles of maintained trails through fields and woods. Rentals,
waxing shelter, maps, use fee.
Directions: Arrive in Andover by best route. Ask in town for
"Akers" Ski Area.

Auburn Ski Touring Center
North River Rd.
Auburn, ME 04210 (Map Key D-2)
Tel. (207) 782-1360
10-15 miles of mixed woods and fields, trails marked for level of
difficulty. Trail map available. No snowmobiles. Snack bar, ren-
tals, instruction, waxing shelter.
Directions: Rt. 4 to Auburn, take North River Road at Wendy's
Hamburger, go 3 miles to Center.

Baxter State Park
Millinocket, ME 04462 (Map Key G-6)
Tel. (207) 723-5140
Open to the more experienced skier in this 200,000-acre wilderness
park are 5 miles of marked and groomed cross-country trails and
150 miles of ungroomed trails, including tote roads. Several
cabins, lean-tos, and tent sites are available in remote areas. Permission for overnight camping must be obtained two weeks in ad-

vance. For further information contact the Baxter State Park headquarters noted above.

Directions: From I-95 take Rt. 11/57 west to Millinocket, go northwest on Park Road, turn right onto Roaring Brook Rd.

Bethel Inn Ski Touring Center
Bethel, ME 04217 (Map Key D-1)
Tel. (207) 824–2175
15 miles of marked and groomed trails. Instruction, rentals, accommodations.

Directions: Travel best route to Bethel. Inn is right in town.

Big Rock Touring Center
Mars Hill, ME 04758 (Map Key I-8)
Tel. (207) 425–6711
Two rolling trails, 3 miles and 1/2 mile. Adjacent to alpine ski area. Instruction, rental. Nearby lodge and restaurant.

Directions: Rt. 1 to Mars Hill, follow Rt. 1A out of town 2 miles to ski area.

The Birches Cross-Country Ski Center
Rockwood, ME 04478 (Map Key G-4)
Tel. (207) 534–7305
25 scenic miles (10 of which are track set) of trails around Moosehead Lake, plus hundreds of miles of logging roads which are skiable. Housekeeping cottages overlooking the lake. Rentals, instruction, waxing facility, maps, tours, base lodge. Restaurant a mile away.

Directions: Travel to Greenville. Take Rt. 15 to Rockwood, cross Moose River Bridge, go 2 miles on gravel road to The Birches.

Black Mountain of Maine
Rumford, ME (Map Key E-2)
Tel. (207) 364–8977
One 4 1/2-mile racing trail through woods. Instructor. Rentals, snack bar, and lounge at adjacent alpine ski area. No fee.

Directions: Arrive in Bethel, take Rt. 2 north to Rumford, watch for signs.

Bradbury Mt. State Park
Pownal, ME 04069 (Map Key C-2)
Tel. (207) 688–4712
2 miles of mixed gentle to steep. Trail ascends the peak 460'. Trail marked, no maps. Snowmobiles not permitted on trails.

Directions: Rt. 9 to Pownal.

Camden Hills State Park
Lincolnville, ME 04849 (Map Key D-5)
Tel. (207) 236–3109
12 miles of trails, novice to intermediate, with excellent views of Penobscot Bay. Trails include old roads and well-marked hiking trails. Some snowmobile use near Ski Lodge and Mt. Battie roads.
Directions: From Lincolnville, go west on Rt. 173, 2.3 miles to Steven's Corner. Bear left onto Youngtown Road. Continue 100 yards to Ski Lodge Road. Park here.

Camden Snow Bowl
P.O. Box 456
Camden, ME 04843 (Map Key D-5)
Tel. (207) 236–4418
Maps at Snow Bowl lead you through fields and wooded areas in the Camden Hills. Lodge, snack bar, rentals, instruction.
Directions: From Rt. 1 in Camden take Hosmer Pond Road for 3 miles to Snow Bowl.

Carrabassett Valley Touring Center
Carrabassett Valley, ME 04947 (Map Key F-3)
Tel. (207) 237–2205
75-mile trail system for novice through expert, with miles of wilderness skiing, including parts of the Appalachian Trail and Bigelow Mountain Preserve. Only one mile from Sugarloaf/USA. Lodge with rentals, repairs, instruction, and cafeteria. Olympic-size skating rink.
Directions: From Kingfield follow Rt. 16/27 north about 15 miles, turn left at sign.

Deer Farm Touring Center
P.O. Box 78
Kingfield, ME 04947 (Map Key F-3)
Tel. (207) 265–2241
30 miles of trails with maps available. Large trail interlocking several thousand acres. No snowmobiles. The 45th parallel is crossed on one trail, allowing you to stand halfway between the Equator and the North Pole! Trails groomed. Deer Farms is connected to Carrabassett Valley Touring Center—lots of room. Ski shop, rentals, wax, guided tours, small trail fee. Heated log cabins available for overnight.
Directions: North from Kingfield on Rt. 16/27 for one mile. Turn left at Deer Farm sign.

Edelweiss Touring Center
Rangeley, ME 04970 (Map Key F-1)
Tel. (207) 864–3891
30 miles of marked and groomed trails. Waxing facility, rentals, instruction, guided tours.
Directions: Located on north shore of Dodge Pond 3 miles west of Rangeley. Suggest arrive in Rangeley and ask specific directions.

Hermon Meadow Ski Center
RFD 2
Bangor, ME 04401 (Map Key E-6)
Tel. (207) 848–3741
Actually a golf course which doubles for ski touring in winter. Trails marked on map. No snowmobiles. Snack bar, rentals, instruction, wax room.
Directions: Hermon exit off I-95, north on Cold Brook Road to Hermon Corner.

Holbrook Island Sanctuary
Brooksville, ME 04617 (Map Key D-6)
Rocky shoreline bordering Penobscot Bay. Easy trails over old roads. Snowmobiles permitted.
Directions: Rt. 1 to Orland, Rt. 175 south to North Brooksville. Look for sign to Cape Rosier.

Katahdin Lake Wilderness Camps
Box 398
Millinocket, ME 04462 (Map Key G-6)
A day-long ski trip from the entrance of Baxter State Park will bring you to one of Maine's most peaceful and remote winter camps. 50 miles of marked trails with overland access to park. Wood-heated cabins and dining lodge, or you can pack in your own supplies. No telephone or road access. Arrangements should be made well in advance by writing to Alfred J. Cooper, III, at the address above.

Little Lyford Pond Camps
Box 688
Brownville, ME 04414 (Map Key C-1)
For a complete cross-country skiing vacation this touring center, accessible only by skis or plane, is a perennially popular wilderness retreat. Only two miles from Gulf Hagas (a scenic gorge), the area offers over 40 miles of trails surrounded by Baker, Elephant, and Whitecap mountains, and numerous ponds. No trail fee, and lim-

ited rentals. Maps and compasses, day packs, guided tours, and instruction are available free of charge. Seven guest cabins are located near a dining lodge and cedar sauna. The daily rate includes meals. Fly-in reservations may be made through Folsom's Air Service in Greenville, Tel. (207) 695-2821, or contact the owners, Joel and Lucy Frantzman at the address above.

Livermore Falls Nordic Ski Assn.
Livermore Falls, ME 04254 (Map Key D-2)
10 mile network of trails at Spruce Mountain alpine ski area, with lodge. Nearby 35-meter jump. Ski rentals in town (1/2 mile from area). Call (207) 897-3191 for conditions.
Directions: Arrive in Livermore Falls, turn west on Rt. 4, cross the Androscoggin River, take first right north to ski area.

Moosehorn National Wildlife Refuge
Calais, ME 04619 (Map Key F-9)
Tel. (207) 454-3521
22,000 acres await you here, in two separate areas. The Baring Division is larger and encompasses the headquarters in Calais. The Edmunds Division, 25 miles south in Edmunds and Dennysville, has a state camping and recreational center. Both ski areas run along coastal landscapes. Good views are limited to the Whiting Bay area. Trails follow gravel roads, are marked, maps available. Snowmobiles allowed only in certain areas. The wildlife areas are xc only. Good idea to call ahead on this one.
Directions: Take Rt. 9 east from Bangor to Calais.

Mt. Abram Ski Slopes
Locke Mills, ME 04255 (Map Key D-1)
Tel. (207) 875-2601
One maintained cross-country trail (no snowmobiles) through hardwoods and evergreens. Some logging roads available. No fee. Rentals available at base lodge.
Directions: Follow Rt. 26 to Locke Mills.

Mt. Blue State Park
Weld, ME 04285 (Map Key E-2)
Tel. (207) 585-2347
15 miles of trails, mixed intermediate and advanced. Expect snowmobile use on weekends. Trail maps available at park H.Q.
Directions: Rt. 4 to Wilton, Rt. 156 northwest to Weld, follow signs to park.

Narrow Gauge XC Trail
Bigelow ME (Map Key F-2)
This trail follows the bed of an old narrow-gauge railroad. Maps
are available at Carrabassett Valley Touring Center. Trail follows
the river. Good game spotting trips.
Directions: Go north from Kingfield on Rt. 16/27, 300 yards past
entrance to Sugarloaf Mt. On right look for cabins near abandoned Bigelow Station. Leave a shuttle car at Valley Crossing
Shopping Center if you plan a one-way trip.

Saddleback Mt. Ski Area
Box 490, Access Road
Rangeley, ME 04970 (Map Key F-1)
Tel. (207) 864–3380
Wooded trails with fine views of Rangeley lakes. Accommoda-
tions close by in Rangeley.
Directions: Follow Rt. 4 toward Rangeley, approximately 1 mile
south of town turn east on the access road, follow signs.

Sebago Lake State Park
Naples, ME 04055 (Map Key C-2)
Tel. (207) 693–6231 (winter)
3-mile loop through hardwoods and evergreens, includes a beach
run. Signs and trail map, some snowmobile use.
Directions: Park located off Rt. 135 between Naples and Ray-
mond.

Squaw Mt. Ski Area
P.O. Box 503
Greenville, ME 04441 (Map Key G-4)
Tel. (207) 695–2272
An alpine ski resort with 15 miles of marked and unmarked xc
trails. Excellent views of Moosehead Lake, Katahdin, and Mt.
Kineo. Rentals and instruction available.
Directions: From Greenville, go north on Rt. 6/15 six miles to
sign.

Sunday River Ski Touring Center
Bethel, ME 04217 (Map Key D-1)
Tel. (207) 824–2410
25-mile network of trails with scenic views of Old Spec Mountain
and Sunday River valley. All trails novice to intermediate. Also,
100 miles of cleared, marked logging roads for more experienced
skiers. Night touring by kerosene lamplight every Friday night.

Season finale race in early April involves skis, canoes, and snowshoes. Lodging, rentals, instruction, maps, tours, waxing facility.

Note: Nordic Nastar races are held every weekend. USSA races throughout the season. Daily use fee.

Directions: Arrive in Bethel, follow signs to area.

Teddy Bear Touring Trails
North Turner, ME 04266 (Map Key D-2)
Tel. (207) 224-8275 or 783-1037
Open weekends and holidays. 10 miles of marked and groomed trails. Instruction, rentals, light snacks. No snowmobiles.

Directions: Rt. 4 to Rt. 219, 15 miles north of Auburn. Turn west onto Rt. 219, one mile to park.

University Forest
Stillwater, ME 04489 (Map Key F-6)
University of Maine uses this as a training course. 3½ miles through forest and meadows through a game preserve. Some snowmobile use.

Directions: Arrive in Orono, proceed to Stillwater, watch for signs.

---

42 Downhill Skiing

The following eight ski areas are the major ski attractions in Maine. Each is served by ample lodging and restaurant facilities, either at the slope or nearby. I would recommend you contact the ski areas themselves for the current rates and availability of lodging. They would be glad to respond.

Camden Snow Bowl
Camden, ME 04843 (Map Key D-5)
Tel. (207) 236-3438
950' vertical drop, 8 miles of terrain
1 chair, 2 T-bars, 20% snowmaking coverage
Where the mountains meet the sea, the Snow Bowl is on 1300'
Ragged Mountain. From the summit there are breathtaking views

197

of Penobscot Bay and the islands. The terrain is varied for all abilities, and the mountain has a day lodge, cross-country skiing, instruction programs, alpine and cross-country rentals, and night skiing. Operated by the Samoset Resort in Rockport, just 10 miles away.

Lost Valley Ski Area
P.O. Box 260
Auburn, ME 04210 (Map Key D-2)
Tel. (207) 784–1561
240' vertical drop, 8 miles terrain
2 chairs, 1 T-bar, 100% snowmaking coverage
A short drive from downtown Lewiston-Auburn, Lost Valley is a great family resort. The ski school is the largest in the state and holds children's classes and adult learn-to-ski programs. Snowmaking (Lost Valley was the first area in the state with snowmaking), night skiing, large rental shop, lounge, and snack shop.

Mt. Abram Ski Slopes
Locke Mills, ME 04255 (Map Key D-1)
Tel. (207) 875–2601
1030' vertical drop, 12 miles of terrain
1 chair, 3 T-bars
Mt. Abram is not the biggest in the state, but is known for its relaxed family atmosphere and meticulously groomed slopes. 13 major trails, covering 100 acres, providing skiing for everyone from novice to mogul-loving experts. For less advanced skiers there's Duane's Retreat, a separate beginners' area with gentle slopes and easy-riding T-bars. 15 miles of groomed cross-country trails are also available.

Services include a ski shop offering sales, service, and rentals for both alpine and cross-country skiers, a P.S.I.A. ski school utilizing the American Teaching Method, junior and racing programs, a cafeteria, and lounge. Lodging is within 10 to 25 minutes of the slopes and all offer special winter packages to skiers.

Pleasant Mountain Ski Area
RFD 1 Box 734
Mountain Road
Bridgton, ME 04022 (Map Key C-1)
Tel. (207) 647–8444
1256' vertical drop, 20 miles of terrain
3 chairs, 3 T-bars
Pleasant Mountain is conveniently located in southwestern Maine,

on Rt. 302 in Bridgton. The resort offers two base lodges, ski shop with rentals, ski school, and summit warming hut. A lift capacity of 4200 skiers per hour means more skiing and short lines at prices that fit your budget.

Saddleback Ski Area
Box 490
Rangeley, ME 04970 (Map Key F-1)
Tel. (207) 864-3380
1800' vertical drop, 15 miles of terrain
2 chairs, 3 T-bars, 90% snowmaking coverage
Located in the heart of the northeast snowbelt, Saddleback Ski Area combines a relaxing atmosphere, unhurried pace, and the breathtaking scenery of the Rangeley Lakes region to provide a complete skiing experience. With a vertical drop of over 1800', Saddleback offers some of the most enjoyable, varied, and challenging skiing in the East, with something for every skiier.

Saddleback features the latest in snowmaking and grooming equipment to insure reliable surface conditions, and specializes in personal treatment. All packages include meals at any area restaurant.

Squaw Mountain at Moosehead
P.O. Box D
Greenville, ME 04441 (Map Key G-4)
Tel. (207) 695-2272
1750' vertical drop, 14 miles of terrain
1 chair, 3 T-bars, 30% snowmaking coverage
Overlooking spectacular Moosehead Lake, Squaw is a great family ski resort. The resort complex located at the base of the lifts includes the full service Squaw Mountain Lodge, indoor pool and sauna, lounge, nursery, game rooms, restaurant, bar, cafeteria, ski school, and ski shop. There are 16 trails for all ability levels, and the ski school has programs for all ages and abilities. Cross-country and snowmobile trails, and fly-in tours are also available.

Sugarloaf/USA
Carrabassett Valley, ME 04947 (Map Key F-3)
Tel. (207) 237-2000
2600' vertical drop, 36 miles of terrain
6 chairs, 4 T-bars, gondola, 50% snowmaking coverage
Sugarloaf/USA is famed as *the* skier's mountain, with terrain ranging from gentle at the base to super-steep off the summit. Snowmaking covers 13 trails, including 4 from the summit, for all

levels of ability. Serviced by 11 lifts, including the gondola.

Sugarloaf/USA has a complete village, replete with lodges, condominiums, restaurants, pubs, shops, and stores. Everything is on the mountain with either foot or ski access—no need for a car.

Services include a modern day care facility (free non-holiday midweeks), a full-service ski shop, ski school, real estate office, and much more.

Sunday River Ski Resort
Box 450
Bethel, ME 04217 (Map Key D-1)
Tel. (207) 824–2187
1630' vertical drop, 15 miles of terrain
2 chairs, 2 T-bars, 1 poma, 45% snowmaking coverage
Sunday River Ski Resort has made a commitment to provide skiing at a sensible and affordable price. Sunday River is one of the best terrain havens in New England with a three-mile novice trail, consistent fall line terrain for intermediates, and explosive bump runs for experts. Sunday River's top-to-bottom snowmaking system covers 70 acres of terrain, and has earned the respect of skiers for 12 years. Services include two base lodges with cafeterias, lounge, day care centers, ski shop with rentals, and ski school with children's program.

Sugarloaf/USA photo.

There are some fine smaller areas scattered about Maine. These less well-known slopes often are free from crowded lift lines and are ideal for the family who skis.

Baker Mt.
Moscow, ME 04920 (Map Key F-3)
Tel. (207) 672–5580
2170′ T-bar with a 1500′ open slope, ski shop, snack bar, instruction, and rentals.

Big Rock
Mars Hill, ME 04758 (Map Key I-8)
Tel. (207) 425–6711
Largest ski area in northern Maine. Poma lift to 1000′, 5 trails, 2 open slopes, lodge, rentals, instruction, 3 miles xc skiing, snack bar.

Black Mt. of Maine
Rumford, ME 04276 (Map Key E-2)
Tel. (207) 364–8977
8 trails, 2 open slopes. Offers night skiing, snack bar, lodge, instruction, 9 miles xc trails.

Colby College Ski Slope
Waterville, ME 04901 (Map Key E-4)
No telephone
T-bars with smaller trails and open slopes, snack bar, night skiing.

Eaton Mt.
Skowhegan, ME 04976 (Map Key E-4)
Tel. (207) 474–2666
2200′ double chair lift, open slopes, ski shop, instruction, lodge, snack bar, night skiing. 4–5 miles xc trails.

Hermon Mt. Ski Area
Hermon, ME 04401 (Map Key E-6)
Tel. (207) 848–5192
2 T-bars 2000′ long, 1 rope tow, 4 major trails, 3 open slopes, instruction, ski shop, rentals, lodge, snack bar, snowmaking, night skiing.

May Mt.
Island Falls, ME 04747 (Map Key H-7)
Tel. (207) 463–2101
T-bars connecting 6 trails, 75 acres open slopes, snack bar, instruction, lodge, night skiing.

Mt. Jefferson
Lee, ME 04455 (Map Key G-7)
Tel. (207) 738-2377
2000′ T-bar, 600′ rope tow, 20 acres open slopes, ski shop, rentals, lodge, snack bar, night skiing.

Northmen Ski Area
Caribou, ME 04736 (Map Key J-8)
No telephone
1000′ T-bar, open slopes, 1 trail, snack bar, lodge, night skiing.

Snow Mt.
Winterport, ME 04496 (Map Key E-6)
No telephone
T-bar to 10 trails, 50 acres open slopes, snack bar, lodge, instruction, rentals, night skiing.

Spruce Mt.
Jay, ME 04239 (Map Key E-2)
Tel. (207) 897-4090
Rope tows to 4 trails and open slopes, snack bar, lodge, instruction, night skiing.

Tater Mt.
Temple, ME 04984 (Map Key E-2)
No telephone
T-bar to 3 trails, 20 acres open slopes, lodge, snack bar, instruction, night skiing.

Titcomb Slope
Farmington, ME 04938 (Map Key E-3)
Tel. (207) 778-9031
2 T-bars, 5 trails, 50 acres open slopes, instruction, lodge, snack bar, night skiing.

■ Snowmobiling

43 Regulations

All snowmobiles operated in Maine must be registered except those used only on land where the operator lives. The registration period is one year beginning in July, and the fee is $11.25. Registration is available from: Snowmobile Section, Maine Department of Inland Fisheries and Wildlife, 284 State St., Station 41, Augusta, ME 04333.

Registration numbers must be at least three inches high, contrast with the color of the machine, and be firmly attached to the cowling. Dealers issue 20-day temporary registrations at the time of sale.

Snowmobiles may cross all roads except controlled access highways. Operators under age 14 cannot cross roads. Snowmobiles can operate between sunrise and sunset on the unused and unplowed right of way parallel to all roads, except controlled access highways. They may operate on all roads which are not plowed or used in winter.

Snowmobiles may not operate on the traveled portion of a public road or its snowbanks, except to cross, on any railroad right of way without written permission, within the grounds of any cemetery, or on any plowed road after having been so notified by the owner.

It is illegal to operate a snowmobile recklessly, while under the influence of liquor, or to endanger any person or property.

All snowmobiles must have an adequate muffler, a headlight capable of casting a white beam for 100 feet in front of the machine, and a red taillight which can be seen at 100 feet. Lights must be used from one half hour after sunset to one half hour before sunrise.

44 Maps and Trails

The State of Maine offers snowmobiling in many State Parks. Information on trails, opening dates, and regulations can be obtained from:

> Snowmobile Division
> Bureau Parks & Recreation
> Station 19
> Augusta, ME 04333

OPEN PARKS

Aroostook (Presque Isle), Camden Hills (Camden), Cobscook Bay (Dennysville), Lake St. George (Liberty), Lily Bay (Greenville), Mt. Blue (Weld), Sebago Lake (Naples), Crescent Beach (Cape Elizabeth), Peaks-Kenny (Dover-Foxcroft), Reid (Georgetown), and Popham Beach (Phippsburg).

TWO BIG EVENTS

Each year the *"Rangeley Snodeo"* in Rangeley, and the world famous *"Log Drivers Cookout"* on Mud Pond, Island Falls are major attractions for snowmobilers. Write Chambers of Commerce for complete details.

Dept. of Conservation Bureau of Parks and Recreation, State Office Building, Augusta, ME 04333. Tel. (207) 289-3821.

Areas covered: Squaw Mt. (Greenville G-4)
Mt. Blue & Rangeley (F-1)
Beddington (E-8)
Island Falls (H-7)

Ask also for the I.T.S. (Interconnected Trail System)

Greenville Chamber of Commerce Box 581, Greenville, ME 04441. Tel. (207) 695-2702. Has excellent map of Moosehead Lake area.

Jackman Chamber of Commerce Jackman, ME 04945. Tel. (207) 235-2100. Ask for map by Stephen Coleman.

Presque Isle Chamber of Commerce Presque Isle, ME 04769. Tel. (207) 764-6561. Ask for snowmobile trail map of "The County."

■ Leisure Activities

45 Moose Watching

Some of you never will be hunters and we won't try to make you into one. So if watching wildlife is your interest, check the following locations. They are excellent places to see "our Maine Moose" which can reach 1200 pounds!

MOOSE WATCHING AREAS

Site	Township	Remarks
AROOSTOOK COUNTY		
Big Machias Lake	T12 R8 WELS	
Pratt Lake	T11 R9 WELS	
Reality Road	Various	Main road and side roads west of Ashland.
Route 11	T7 R5 WELS	Between Knowles Corner and the Oxbow turn-off.
St. Croix Lake	T8 R4 WELS	Off Route 11 easterly about 4 miles north of Knowles Corner.
FRANKLIN COUNTY		
Chesterville Wildlife Management Area	Chesterville	
Route 4	Phillips and Madrid	Phillips to Madrid.
Webb Lake	Weld	At the head of the lake.
OXFORD COUNTY		
Grafton Flats	Grafton	Large mud hole beside Route 26 at the end of the old airport.
SOMERSET COUNTY		
Luther Pond Outlet	Thorndike Twp.	
Mose Holden Pond	Dennistown	Route 201
Route 201	Johnson Mtn. Twp.	From Markham Brook to Young's Flying Service at Lake Parlin.

MOOSE WATCHING AREAS

Site	Township	Remarks
SOMERSET COUNTY (*cont'd*)		
Route 201	Parlin Pond Twp.	Bean Brook Crossing.
PISCATAQUIS COUNTY		
Brighton Deadwater	T3 R12 WELS T4 R11 WELS	Along Ripogenus Stream. Can be reached by a short walk from forestry campsite along a 4WD road.
Caribou Stream	T2 R12 WELS	At south end of Caribou Lake right beside the Golden Road.
Churchill Dam	T10 R12 WELS	Accessible only by boat.
Dwelley Pond*	T5 R10 WELS	Accessible by vehicle. Frequently seen in Baxter State Park Picnic Area.
East Road to Thissel Pond	T5 R11 WELS	From Great Northern Camps one mile north of town line.
1st and 2nd West Branch Ponds	TA R12 WELS	
Grassy Pond*	T3 R10	One mile hike from Katahdin Stream Campground.

*Located in Baxter State Park.

46 Golf Courses

For you divot diggers the following list should provide an ample variety. Plan a travel route through Maine so you touch down at a convenient course. Nice way to explore Maine by car and relax.

27 HOLES

Portland
Riverside Municipal Course   Riverside St. 18-hole course 6,502 yd., par 72; 9-hole course 3,152 yd., par 36. Tel. (207) 797–3524.

18 HOLES

Arundel
Dutch Elm Golf Course   RR 4 Brimstone Rd. 6,400 yd., par 72. Carts, snack bar. Tel. (207) 282–9850.

Auburn
Martindale Country Club   6,376 yd., par 71. Carts, dining bar, grill. Members only and their guests. Tel. (207) 782–9074.

Prospect Hill Golf Course   694 S. Main Street, 5,900 yd., par 71. Restaurant, putting greens, carts. Tel. (207) 782–9220.

Bangor
Bangor Municipal Golf Course   Webster Ave. 6,500 yd., par 72. Driving range, snack bar. Tel. (207) 945–9226.

Bar Harbor
Kebo Valley Golf Club   Eagle Lake Road, 6,209 yd., par 70. Carts and snack bar. Tel. (207) 288–3000.

Cape Elizabeth
Purpoodock Club   Spurwink Ave. 6,021 yd., par 70. Caddies, clubhouse, carts. Visitor play restricted to weekdays. Tel. (207) 799–1574.

East Poland
Fairlawn Golf Course   6,440 yd., par 72. Snack bar, cocktail bar, carts. Tel. (207) 998–4277.

Falmouth
Portland Country Club (strictly private)   Foreside Rd. 6,488 yds., par 71. Carts, pool, tennis. Tel. (207) 781-3053.

Fort Fairfield
Aroostook Valley Country Club   6,403 yd., par 72. Caddies, carts, grills. Tel. (207) 476-6501.

Gorham
Gorham Country Club McLellan Rd. 6,509 yd., par 71. Clubhouse, grill. Tel. (207) 839-3490.

Hermon
Hermon Meadow Golf Club   Rt. 2, 6,270 yd., par 72. Pro shop, snack bar. Tel. (207) 848-3741.

Kennebunk Beach
Webhannet Golf Club   6,031 yd., par 70. Caddies, carts, clubhouse. Tel. (207) 967-2061.

Kennebunkport
Cape Arundel Golf Club   5,900 yd., par 69. Caddies, clubhouse, golf shop. Tel. (207) 967-3494.

Leeds
Springbrook Golf Course   Rt. 202, 6,700 yd., par 71. Pro shop, restaurant, carts, motel. Tel. (207) 933-4551.

Manchester
Augusta Country Club   Rt. 202, 6,200 yd., par 70. Pro shop, carts, dining. Tel. (207) 623-3021.

Orono
Penobscot Valley Country Club   6,301 yd., par 72. Carts, bar, grill, clubhouse. Tel. (207) 866-2423.

Poland Spring
Poland Spring Country Club   6,731 yd., par 71. Carts, clubhouse, grill, bar, swimming pool, tennis, and lodging. Tel. (207) 998-4352.

Rangeley
Mingo Springs Golf Course   off Route 4 & Mingo Loop Rd. 6,000 yd., par 70. Carts & clubs. Tel. (207) 864-5021.

Rockland
Rockland Golf Club Inc.   Old Country Rd. 6,300 yd., par 70. Restaurant & bar, carts, lessons. Tel. (207) 594-9322.

Rockport
Samoset Resort   Warrenton St. 6,285 yd., par 70. Pools, health club, saunas. Tel. (207) 594-2511.

Scarborough
Willowdale Golf Club off US Rt. 1, 5,980 yd., par 70. Carts, grill. Tel. (207) 883-9351.

Trenton
Bar Harbor Golf Course Jct. Rts. 3 and 204, 6,720 yd., par 72. Clubhouse, pro shop, dining. Tel. (207) 667-7505.

Vassalboro
Natanis Golf Course Webber Pond Rd. 5,935 yd., par 71. Tennis courts. Tel. (207) 622-3561.

Waterville
Waterville Country Club off I-95, 6,390 yd., par 69. Caddies, carts, clubhouse, grill. Tel. (207) 465-7773.

Westbrook
Ponderosa Park Cumberland St. 1,305 yd., par 54. Driving range. Tel. (207) 854-9463.

York
York Golf & Tennis Club Organug Rd. 6,159 yd., par 70. Tennis courts. Tel. (207) 363-2683.

9 HOLES

Augusta
Western View Golf Club, Inc. Bolton Hill Rd. 2,705 yd., par 35. Bar, clubhouse, driving range. Tel. (207) 622-5309.

Bath
Bath Country Club Whiskeag Rd. 3,213 yd., par 35. Carts, clubhouse, range, pro shop, bar, grill. Tel. (207) 443-5735.

Bethel
Bethel Inn & Country Club Broad St. 3,105 yd., par 36. Inn, dining room, lounge. Tel. (207) 824-2969.

Boothbay
Boothbay Region Country Club Country Club Rd. 2,625 yd., par 35. Bar & grill. Tel. (207) 633-6085.

Brewer
Woodland Terrace Motel & Golf Course 1,600 yd., par 30. Motel, pool, shuffleboard. Tel. (207) 989-3750.

Pine Hill Golf Club Brewer Lake Ave. 2,863 yd., par 36. Tel. (207) 989-8814.

Bridgton
Bridgton Highlands Country Club Highland Ridge, 3,212 yd., par 37. Clubhouse, snack bar, carts. Tel. (207) 647-3491.

Brooks
Country View Golf Club 2,856 yd., par 36. Snack bar, pro-shop, clubs, carts. Tel. (207) 722-3161.

Bucksport
Bucksport Golf & Country Club Duckscove Rd. 3,382 yd., par 36. Snack bar, carts, driving range. Tel. (207) 469-7612.

Camden
Goose River Golf Course Simonton Rd. 2,856 yd., par 35. Snack bar, clubs, carts, pro shop. Tel. (207) 236-8488.

Caribou
Caribou Country Club New Sweden Rd. 3,206 yd., par 36. Clubhouse. Tel. (207) 493-3933.

Carmel
Carmel Valley Golf Club 1,258 yd., par 27. Snack bar. Tel. (207) 848-5237.

Castine
Castine Golf Club Battle Ave. 3,044 yd., par 35. Tennis courts, clubhouse, pro shop. Tel. (207) 326-4221.

Chebeague Island
Great Chebeague Golf Club 3,295 yd., par 33. Tel. (207) 846-9478.

Cumberland
Val Halla Golf Club 3,323 yd., par 36. Lounge, food, carts, tennis. Tel. (207) 829-3700.

Deer Isle
Island Country Club 1,856 yd., par 31. Clubhouse, grill. Tel. (207) 348-2379.

Dexter
Dexter Municipal Golf Club Sunrise Ave. 2,586 yd., par 35. Pro shop, lunches, carts. Tel. (207) 924-6477.

Dover-Foxcroft
Foxcroft Golf Club Milo Rd. 2,922 yd., par 36. Clubs, carts, lunch counter.

Ellsworth
White Birches Golf Course 2,600 yd., par 33. Restaurant, motel,

lounge, tennis. Tel. (207) 667-5682.

Enfield
Green Valley Golf Course 2,624 yd., par 35. Lunch room. Tel. (207) 732-3006.

Farmingdale
Meadowhill Golf Club US 201, 3,112 yd., par 36. Sundeck, carts, rentals, snack bar, beer on draft. Tel. (207) 623-9831.

Fort Kent
Fort Kent Golf Club St. John Rd. 3,160 yd., par 36. Caddies, carts, clubhouse, grill. Tel. (207) 834-3149.

Freeport
Freeport Country Club Rt. 1. 3,000 yd., par 36. Carts, grill, clubhouse. Tel. (207) 865-4922.

Greenville
Squaw Mountain Village on Moosehead Lake 2,563 yd., par 34. Lounge, restaurant, private beach. Tel. (207) 695-3049.

Guilford
Piscataquis Country Club Dover Rd. 2,855 yd., par 34. Carts, clubhouse, grill, pro-shop, lessons. Tel. (207) 876-3203.

Hampden
Hampden Country Club Western Ave. par 36. Pro shop, carts, clubs. Tel. (207) 862-9999.

Hartford
Green Acres Inn 2,050 yd., par 31. Cabins, dining room. Tel. (207) 597-2281

Hollis
Salmon Falls Restaurant-Motel & Golf Club Salmon Falls Rd. Off Rt. 202. 2,752 yd., par 35. Restaurant, lounge, motel, pool, snack bar. Tel. (207) 929-5233.

Island Falls
Va-Jo-Wa Golf Course Walker Rd. 3,275 yd., par 36. Pro shop, clubhouse, lounge. Tel. (207) 463-2128.

Islesboro
Tarratine Golf Club Golf Club Rd. 3,085 yd., par 37. Carts, pro shop. Tel. (207) 734-2248.

Kenduskeag
Kenduskeag Valley Golf Course Rt. 15, 2,562 yd., par 34.

Lewiston
Apple Valley Golf Course Pinewoods Rd. 2,500 yd., par 36.

Snack bar, pro shop, carts, clubs. Tel. (207) 784-9773.

Livermore Falls
Maple Lane Golf Course 2,704 yd., par 35. Pro shop, restaurant. Tel. (207) 897-5855.

Lovell
Lake Kezar Country Club Rt. 5, 2,988 yd., par 36. Clubhouse, carts. Tel. (207) 925-2462.

Madawaska
Birch Point Golf Club Lakeshore Dr. 3,682 yd., par 35. Pro shop, lounge, game room.

Madison
Lakewood Golf Course Rt. 201, 3,087 yd., par 36. Clubs, carts, bar. Tel. (207) 474-5955.

Mexico
Oakdale Country Club Rt. 2, 3,050 yd., par 35. Clubhouse, pro shop, lunch counter, bar. Tel. (207) 364-3951.

Millinocket
Hillcrest Golf Club 2,500 yd., par 33. Snack bar. Tel. (207) 723-8410.

Milo
Katahdin Country Club Park St. 3,000 yd., par 36. Clubhouse, grill, carts.

Monmouth
Cobbossee Colony Golf Course 2,488 yd., par 34. Clubhouse, self-service food & drink. Tel. (207) 268-4182.

Moose River
Moose River Golf Course 2,100 yd., par 31. Dining, lodging, clubs, carts.

North Haven
North Haven Club 3,040 yd., par 35. Carts, clubs, clubhouse.

Northport
Northport Golf Club 3,047 yd., par 36. Carts, clubhouse. Tel. (207) 338-2270.

Norway
Norway Country Club 2,741 yd., par 35. Snack bar, clubs, carts, pro shop. Tel. (207) 743-9840.

Newport
Sebasticook Golf Club Old Corinna Rd. 2,240 yd., par 30. Lunch counter.

Ogunquit
Cliff Country Club Shore Rd. 2,912 yd., par 36. Snack bar, carts. Tel. (207) 646-7724.

Old Orchard Beach
Old Orchard Beach Country Club Cascade & Ross Rd. Rte. 98, 3,006 yd., par 36. Snack bar, pro shop, carts, open to public. Tel. (207) 934-4513.

Palmyra
Grandview Golf Course 3,087 yd., par 35. Driving range. Tel. (207) 938-4947.

Paris
Paris Hill Country Club 2,305 yd., par 33. Pro shop, snack bar, lounge. Tel. (207) 743-2371.

Parsonsfield
Province Lake Country Club Rt. 153, 3,350 yd., par 37. Restaurant, lounge. Tel. (207) 793-9577.

Pittsfield
Johnson W. Parks Golf Course Hartland Ave. 3,000 yd., par 35. Snack bar, carts, clubs.

Poland
Summit Golf Course 2,968 yd., par 36. Tel. (207) 998-4515.

Portage
Woodsman's Country Club Rt. 11N, 3,268 yd., par 37. Clubhouse. Tel. (207) 435-6123.

Presque Isle
Presque Isle Country Club 3,140 yd., par 36. Clubhouse. Tel. (207) 769-7431.

Rockport
Megunticook Golf Club 2,454 yd., par 34. Snack bar, carts. Public plays spring & fall. Tel. (207) 236-2666.

Saco
Biddeford-Saco Country Club Old Orchard Rd. 3,124 yd., par 35. Clubhouse. Tel. (207) 282-5883.

Sanford
Sanford Golf Club 3,294 yd., par 36. Clubhouse, bar, restaurant. Tel. (207) 324-9712.

Scarborough
Pleasant Hill Country Club Chamberlain Rd. 2,400 yd., par 34. Snack bar. Tel. (207) 883-9380.

Spring Valley Country Club   Gorham Rd. Rte 114. 3,200 yd., par 36. Pro shop, carts, drinks. Public invited. Tel. (207) 839-6795.

South Portland
South Portland Municipal Golf Course   Rt. 9, 2,285 yd., par 33. Tennis courts. Public invited. Tel. (207) 775-0005.

Southwest Harbor
Causeway Club   2,300 yd., par 31. Pro shop. Tel. (207) 244-3780.

Stoneham
Evergreen Valley   3,187 yd., par 36. Lodge, pool, tennis, clubs. Tel. (207) 928-3300.

Union
Union Country Club   2,446 yd., par 29.

Walpole
Wawenock Country Club   Rt. 129, 3,161 yd., par 35. Snack bar. Tel. (207) 563-3938.

Waterville
Pine Ridge Golf Course   West River Rd. 1,285 yd., par 27. Tel. (207) 873-0474.

Westbrook
River Meadow Golf Course   Lincoln St. 2,839 yd., par 35. Tel. (207) 854-9071.

Twin Falls Golf Club   Spring St. 2,440 yd. par 33. Snack bar, pro shop, bar. Tel. (207) 854-5397.

Wilton
Wilson Lake Country Club   Weld Rd. 3,116 yd., par 35. Snack bar, pro shop. Tel. (207) 645-2016.

Winter Harbor
Grindstone Neck Golf Course   3,200 yd., par 36. Tel. (207) 963-7760.

15 HOLES

Northeast Harbor
Northeast Harbor Golf Club   4,457 yd., par 57. Tel. (207) 276-5335.

*Carrabassett Valley, 18 hole Championship, under construction by Robert Trent Jones. Par 72, 6,955 yd. for 18 . . . will be playable 1985.

47 Scenic Drives

Who was it that said, "Everybody has to be some place?" I guess for this section I'll have to assume you are somewhere in Maine and just direct you to a starting point.

THE LOOP
(Bethel to Oquossoc, Errol to Bethel)

Start this scenic drive at Bethel (Map Key D-1). Drive north on Rt. 2 through Newry to Rumford. Cross the bridge to Mexico, then north on Rt. 17 to Byron. Back-country Maine will unroll. Stay in Byron to look over Coos Canyon, a small gorge hollowed and polished by the Swift River. Travel north to point where Appalachian Trail crosses Rt. 17. A fantastic view of Mooselookmeguntic Lake unfolds on the driver's left. Continue north to Oquossoc, a small crossroad of fishermen and summer residents. Go left here on Rt. 16 to the dam at Aziscohos Lake, dip briefly into New Hampshire to Errol. Turn south on Rt. 26. Some very scenic mountain vistas unfold as you drive through Grafton Notch. Return on Rt. 26 to Bethel. The Bethel Inn, Box 49, Main Street, Bethel, ME 04217, Tel. (207) 824–2175 should make a good base for The Loop.

CARRABASSETT VALLEY

Arrive in Farmington (Map Key E-3), home of the University of Maine at Farmington. Go north on Rt. 4 to Fairbanks. Don't blink here or you'll miss the turn onto Rt. 27. This road leads to Kingfield and the beautiful Carrabassett Valley. Some excellent river vistas. Plan a stopover at Sugarloaf Mt. Ski Area and a gondola ride to the top of the largest ski mountain in the Northeast. Call ahead to be sure the lift is running, Tel. 1 (800) 343-4075.

The Sugarloaf Inn Resort, Carrabassett Valley, ME 04947, could be a good base of operations for your drive. They have package plans that may appeal to you. (Rafting, canoeing, backpacking available.)

Drive north out of the valley to Stratton. As you cross the bridge just north of town, you'll see a "flowage" caused by a dam on the Dead River. This flowage now covers a town that was once called Flagstaff. The lake now bears this name.

Keep a sharp eye out as you approach Eustis. Watch for a left hand turn marked "Eustis Ridge." A short drive will bring you to a high knoll with a heart stopping view of Bigelow Mt., Flagstaff, and the surrounding country. Be sure to pick a clear, sharp day for this trip. If you are tenting, plan to overnight at Cathedral Pines just south of Eustis. If a history buff, continue north. You'll see sections of the Upper Dead River.

Picnic at Sarampus Falls. Benedict Arnold traveled up this river with some 2,000 men pulling laden, leaking bateaux on his ill-fated attempt to capture Quebec during the American Revolution. His journey is the main theme for Kenneth Robert's book, *Arundel*. The Canadian border beckons just north of Chain of Ponds. If you are returning south, I would suggest you take Route 16 from Stratton over to Rangeley, the heart of famous salmon and trout fishing. You may want to stay overnight with Paul and Barbara Ellis at The Farm House, Rangeley, ME 04970, Tel. (207) 864-3446.

MOOSE WATCH
Come to Greenville (Map Key G-4). You might want to use Leisure Lodge, Greenville ME 04441, Tel. (207) 695-3737

as a base. Ron Masure, who owns the lodge, is a good man to yak with if you are a salmon fisherman. In Greenville there are several flying services that offer quick sightseeing rides. These are well worth it. They often can spot moose from the air.

So now your flight is over, you have two choices.

1. Drive west and north on Rt. 6/15 to Rockwood. Outstanding view of Mt. Kineo will leap right out of Moosehead Lake. The Kineo flint was "mined" and carried all over Maine by Indian tribes. The flint made excellent arrowheads, axes and scrapers. For years a steamer plied the lake and a massive hotel and golf course flourished at the base of the mountain. Lots of local color around Rockwood, particularly if you nose about just north of Rockwood in Moosehorn. Good chance to cross over the river here and follow signs to *The Birches* on Mooshead Lake. These cabins, snuggled in a dense grove of birches, are right on the shore of Moosehead Lake. Stop in or stay over with the John Willard family who offer year-round accommodations and exciting outdoor adventures. *The Birches,* Rockwood, ME 04478, Tel. (207) 534-7305.

2. Head north on Lily Bay Rd. You may want to swing into Lily Bay State Park and check it out for some future camping trip.

Now get out your moose eyes. As you see Elephant Mountain off to the right, you are in the heart of moose country. Just above Kokadjo the road turns to gravel. It can be dusty. The foot of Caribou Lake offers good dri-ki picking. Continue to Ripogenus Dam. This hydroelectric dam controls water from a vast watershed and marks the beginning of the lower West Branch of the Penobscot. Grab a snack at Pray's Store. Pray's Big Eddy Campsite marks one of the northeast's best salmon pools. The road parallels the West Branch for the next eight miles. Take this slow and walk down short logging roads to the river.

Dig out the camera! Abol bridge, where the West Branch crosses, provides one of the best locations in Maine for photographs of Mt. Katahdin, the tallest mountain in Maine and the terminus for those hiking the Appalachian Trail. The entrance to Baxter State Park is just a short drive from Abol bridge. However, very little can be seen from the park itself unless you plan to climb the mountain.

Drive out of the wilderness at Millinocket, home of Great Northern Paper Company. Unlike the famous *Bert & I* record which asks—"Which way to East Millinocket . . . come to think of it, you can't get there from here," you pick up either Rt. 11 or I-95 south to your destination.

COASTAL

Follow Rt. 1 to Ellsworth, then south on Rt. 3 to Mt. Desert Island (pronounced like the dessert that follows a meal). Stop at the information booth on the right just after you cross over the bridge. Very helpful data here. Ask about Sand Beach, The Thunderhole, Somes Sound (a fiord), and Cadillac Mountain. Be sure to allow time to swing into very "Down East" towns of Southwest and Northeast Harbor . . . steamed lobsters!

If a storm is brewing, grab the camera again and head back to Ellsworth, turn right on Rt. 1 to West Gouldsboro, south on Rt. 186 to Winter Harbor and finally to Schoodic Point. Massive waves pound in desperate fury on rocky shores.

Places to stay abound in all these areas. Just pick one.

AIR

Photo by Bill Cross, courtesy of Maine Fish & Game Department.

48 Air Facilities

"Augusta Radio this is N4942Bravo, 5 miles southwest, inbound for landing, request advisory." Every time I thumb down the mike button it ignites all the latent fires of the little boy in me that always wanted to fly. In some of our smaller airfields a call like the one above may be met with a polite silence, which means no one's there at the mike, or they're armpit deep inside an engine and figure if you are in Maine you sure ought to be able to find their field.

This guide will give a ready reference. As any pilot knows, frequencies, VOR's, etc. can change, but runways seldom do. And it's funny about their altitude—always the same! Come visit Maine with your plane. We like having you.

AIRPORTS

Not to be used for navigation—refer to FAA
Flight Charts—Halifax & Montreal

Surface Legend: G = gravel or grass
H = paved surface
* = Lights upon request

Legend:
S2 = Minor airplane repair
S3 = Minor airplane repair & minor power plant
S4 = Major airplane & minor power plant
S5 = Major airplane & major power plant
F.T.L. = Fuel, transportation and lodging within 2 miles of airport.

Airfield	El	Run-ways	Length	Sur-face	Lights	Radio	VOR	CT	Service	F.T.L.	Tel.	Map Key
Augusta State	353'	35-17 26-8	L5149 L2796	H H	On request	F 123.6	111.4		F-100J S5	Yes	289-3185	D-3
Auburn-Lewiston	292'	35-17 22-4	L2750 L5000	H H	Key 3 times	U-122.8			F80-100J S5	Yes	784-5408	CD-2
Bangor-International	102'	33-15	L11440	H		TWR 120.7 9KD 121.9	114.8	Yes	F80-100J S5	Yes	947-0381	E-6
Bar Harbor Hancock	84'	35-17 22-4	2770 *L5196	H	Key 3 times	U-122.8			F-100J S5	Yes	667-7171	D-7
Belfast	197'	33-15	L4000	H	Key 3 times	U-122.8			F80-100 S5	Yes	338-2970	D-5
Biddeford	162'	24-6	L3000	H		U-123.0			F80-100 S5	Yes	282-3713	B-2
Brewer	100'	19-1	L1700	G	On request	122.1	114.8		F100 S5	No	989-1026	E-6
Carrabassett	885'	35-17	2800	H		U-122.8			F100	Yes	235-2288	F-2
Caribou	623'	19-1 29-11	3000 L3435	H H	Key U 3 times	U-122.8			F80-100 S5	Yes	496-7601	J-8
Dexter	533'	34-16 25-7	L3000 1800	H G					F80-100	Yes	924-8822	EF-5
Eliot	130'	30-12	L2500	H	On request	U-122.8			F80-100 S5	Yes	439-4922	A-1

Airfield	El	Runways	Length	Surface	Lights	Radio	VOR	CT	Service	F.T.L.	Tel.	Map Key
Fort Fairfield	470'	26-8	1800	G						Food	473-7114	J-8
Frenchville	988'	32-14	L4000	H	Key U 7 times	U-122.8			F80-100	No	543-7322	K-7
Fryeburg	445'	32-14	L3000	L	On request	U-122.8			F80-100 S5	No	935-2500	C-1
Greenville	1400'	32-14	L3000	H	On request	U-122.8			5-100J S5	Yes	695-2475	G-4
Harrison	570'	36-18	2400	G							887-2862	CD-1
Houlton	493'	23-5	L5000	T	On request	123.6	116.1		F80-100J S5	Yes	532-6223	HI-8
Jackman	1170'	30-12	L2100	H	On request				F-100	Yes	668-2111	G-2
Limington	280'	29-11	3000	H		U-122.8			F80-100 S5	Yes	637-2121	BC-1
Lincoln	208'	35-17	L2800	H	Key U 7 times	U-122.8			F100 S5	Yes	794-3356	F-7
Lubec	85'	26-8	L2032	G	Voice on U	U-122.8				Yes	733-5571	E-10
Machias	100'	36-18	L3000	H	Key U 3 times	U-122.8			F80-100	Yes	255-8709	E-9
Millinocket	408'	29-16	L5000	H	Key U 5 times	U-122.8	117.9		F-100	Yes	723-6649	GH-6

Town	Elev.	Runway	Length	Lighting	Unicom/CTAF	122.8	Freq.	Fuel	Attendant	Phone	Grid
Newport	300'	19-1	2000	G				F-80 S5	Yes	368-5855	E-5
Norway	346'	33-15	L3000	H	On request	U-122.8		F80-100 S5	No	539-9692	D-1,2
Norridge-wock	270'	35-15	L4000	H	Key U	U-122.8		F80-100 S5	No	634-5351	E-3
Old Town	126'	22-4 / 30-12	L4000 / L3600	H / H	Key U 7 times	U-122.8		F80-100J S5	Yes	827-5911	EF-6
Pittsfield	206'	19-1 / 28-10	L4000 / 4000	H / H	Key U	U-122.8		F80-100J S5	Yes	487-5213	E-4
Portland	66'	29-11 / 36-18	L6800 / L5000	H / H	On request		120.9	F80-100J S5	Yes	774-7301	BC-2
Presque Isle	534'	28-10 / 19-1	L5996 / L7440	H / H	Key 122.6	122.8	116.4	F80-100J S5	Yes	764-4485	JI-8
Princeton	266'	33-15 / 24-6	L4000 / 4000	H / H	Key 122.8	122.8	114.3		No	796-2355	F-8
Rangeley	1822'	32-14	2700	H				F80-100 on request	No	864-3347	EF-1
Rockland	55'	21-3 / 31-13	L4000 / L4502	H / H		122.8		F80-100J S5	Yes	594-4131	CD-5
Twitchell's	356'	30-12	2300	H		122.8		F80-100 S5	Yes	225-3490	D-2,3
Waterville	332'	23-5 / 32-14	L5000 / L2300	H / H				F100J S5	Yes	872-5555	DE-4
Wiscasset	68'	25-7	L3400	H	Key U 7 times	122.8		F80-100 S5	Yes	882-5089	C-4

SEA PLANE BASES

Name	El	Length	Radio	Map Key
Twitchell's Turner	255′	10,000	122.8	D-2,3
Folsom's Greenville	1028′	6,000	122.8	G-4
Scotty's Shin Pond	780′	10,500	122.8	HI-6
Millinocket Lake	488′	5,000		GH-6
Rangeley	1578′	15,000	122.8	EF-1
Jackman	1157′	10,000		G-2
Naples	267′	25,000		C-1

SMALLER, LOWER USE AIRFIELDS

Name	El	Runway	Length	Surface	Service	Map Key
Bethel	654′	30-12	2400	G	F80-53	D-1
Bowman	327′	30-12 Approx.	2400	G		D-2,3
Bowdoinham	65′	32-14	2000	G		G-3
Carmel	340′	34-16	1100	G		E-5
Moose River (Sky Lodge)	1350′	27-9	1700	G		G-2

HOT AIR BALLOONING

Balloon Drifters, Inc.
  Augusta State Airport, Augusta, ME 04330, Tel. (207) 622-1211
Sales Aloft,
  North Whitefield, ME 04353, Tel. (207) 549-7483

49 Bush Pilots

Maine has pilots with safe, enviable reputations. I fly floats, skis, and tail draggers for fun and to get myself into the "easier places." My hat is off to these pilots who really know how to fly. They do this flying in all kinds of weather but adhere to the pilots creed, "There are old pilots and there are bold pilots . . . but there are no old, bold pilots!"

Maine bush pilots are experienced fliers who call on years of experience to land on and take off from inaccessible lakes and ponds. Wind, humidity, temperature all play a key role in the "getting in—and getting out!"

All will fly canoes for you and provide airport connections. Some provide rentals or will shuttle cars to the take out point. A call or letter to them will confirm their current operation.

FLYING SERVICES

Name and Address	Canoe Rental	Car Shuttle	Map Key
Air-Tech Aviation Corp. Peter Briggs, Presque Isle Mun. Airport, Presque Isle, ME 04769, Tel. (207) 764-3368 or 764-3100		x	J-8
Currier Flying Service Roger Currier, Box 350, Birch St., Greenville, ME 04441, Tel. (207) 695-3794 or 695-2778	x	x	G-4
Daigle's Flying Service RFD #2, Box 1145, Fort Kent, ME 04743, Tel. (207) 834-5313		x	K-6

Name and Address	Canoe Rental	Car Shuttle	Map Key
Folsom's Air Service Dick & Mary Folsom, Greenville, ME 04441, Tel. (207) 695-2993	x	x	G-4
Jack's Air Service Box 584, Greenville, ME 04441, Tel. (207) 695-3020	x	x	G-4
Millinocket Lake Flying Service Summer: Box 171, Millinocket, ME 04462, Tel. (207) 723-8378; Winter: Mike Higgens, RFD #1, Box 2059, Hampden, ME 04444, Tel. (207) 234-2059	x	x	G-6
Moosehead Flying Service Ramona Morrell (She's the only lady bush pilot.), Box 320, Greenville Jct., ME 04442, Tel. (207) 695-3345	x	x	G-4
Penobscot Flying Service Ross Wheaton, Box 276, Lincoln, ME 04457, Tel. (207) 794-3356 (Bass fisherman check out.)			G-6
Portage Lake Flying Service Clair Moreau, Portage, ME 04765, Tel. (207) 435-0717	x	x	J-7
Porter's Flying Service Dean Wambolat, P.O. Box 269 (Shin Pond) Patten, ME 04765, Tel. (207) 528-2524	x	x	H-6
Scotty's Flying Service Richard Skinner, RFD #1, Box 256, Patten, ME 04765, Tel. (207) 528-2626	x	x	H-6
Steve's Air Service Steve Bean, Box 367, Rangeley, ME 04970, Tel. (207) 864-5307	x	x	F-1
Valley Airlines P.O. Box 88, Frenchville, ME 04745, Tel. (207) 543-7322		x	K-7

GENERAL INFORMATION

50 Who to Call

1. **Acadia National Park**   Tel. (207) 289–3821
2. **Allagash Wilderness Waterway**   Tel. (207) 289–3821
3. **Baxter State Park**   Tel. (207) 723–5140
4. **Boating Regulations**   Tel. (207) 289–2043 (Licensing Division) for both salt & fresh water
5. **Game Warden HQ**   Tel. (207) 289–2766
6. **Hatcheries**   Tel. (207) 289–3651
7. **Hunting & Fishing Regulations**   Tel. (207) 289–2871
8. **Maine Campground Owners Association**   Tel. (207) 782–5874

9. **Maine Publicity Bureau**   Tel. (207) 289–2423
10. **Marine Resources Warden HQ**   Tel. (207) 289–2291
11. **North Maine Woods Association**   Tel. (207) 435–6213
12. **Parks and Recreation**   Tel. (207) 289–3821
13. **Snowmobiles**   Tel. (207) 622–6983 or 289–3821
14. **State Police HQ**   Tel. (207) 289–2155

51 Warden Service

Since members of the warden service frequently change
districts, the list of Regional Headquarters will be more
helpful. Place a toll free call to the HQ nearest your
planned activity. This headquarters will put you in touch
with the local warden for any questions you might have
regarding laws and regulations affecting hunting and
fishing. They are excellent resource people for up-to-date
information on water levels, backwoods road conditions,
washed out bridges, etc.

REGIONAL HEADQUARTERS
GAME WARDENS

Ashland	(toll free) 1–800–322–4011
Augusta	(toll free) 1–800–322–3606
Bangor	(toll free) 1–800–322–2033
Gray	(toll free) 1–800–322–1333
Greenville	(toll free) 1–800–322–9844

If you are unable to locate a warden at one of
the above headquarters, contact the Department
office in Augusta, Tel. (207) 289–2766.

52 Wild Animal Tracks

Many hunters and non-hunters alike enjoy identifying the wild animal tracks they find. This guide should help you fulfill this interest.

(DIRECTION OF TRAVEL OF ALL TRACKS IS TO THE RIGHT)

1. CANADA LYNX
2. BOBCAT
3. HOUSE CAT
4. RED FOX
5. DOG
6. COYOTE
7. BLACK BEAR
8. GRAY SQUIRREL
9. RED SQUIRREL
10. CHIPMUNK
11. WEASEL
12. FISHER
13. MARTEN
14. MINK

R. FRONT   R. HIND

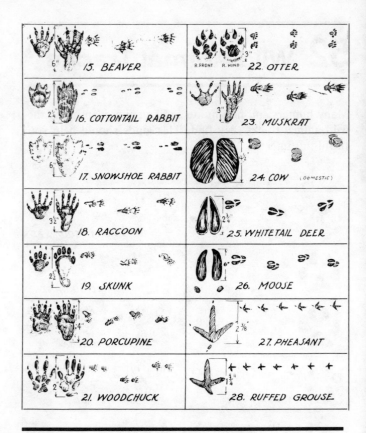

15. BEAVER

16. COTTONTAIL RABBIT

17. SNOWSHOE RABBIT

18. RACCOON

19. SKUNK

20. PORCUPINE

21. WOODCHUCK

22. OTTER
R.FRONT R.HIND

23. MUSKRAT

24. COW (DOMESTIC)

25. WHITETAIL DEER

26. MOOSE

27. PHEASANT

28. RUFFED GROUSE

53 Taxidermists

We often hunt and fish years for that one moment we would like to preserve, to isolate in time, capturing the excitement forever.

The taxidermists listed below are creative Maine people who would like to assist you in trophy mounting.

Antler Taxidermy
Nelson J. Smith
RFD #1, Box 151
Canton, ME 04221
Tel. (207) 597-3283

Taxidermist Gene Bahr
Rt. 107, Hillside Sebago
Box 250-A, East
Baldwin, ME 04024
Tel. (207) 625-8150

B & D Taxidermy
774 River Road
Mexico, ME 04257
Tel. (207) 562-7617

Call of the Wild Taxidermy
RFD #1, Box 1535
Skowhegan, ME 04976
Tel. (207) 474-5593

Central Maine Taxidermy
RFD #1, Box 1090
Vassalboro, ME 04989
Tel. (207) 445-2786

Creative Maine Taxidermy
RFD #1, Box 2092
Kennebunk, ME 04043
Tel. (207) 499-2680

Flying Point Taxidermy Studio
Flying Point Road
P.O. Box 285
Freeport, ME 04032
Tel. (207) 865-3570

Dave Footer
Golder Road
Lewiston, ME 04240
Tel. (207) 783-3501

Reimond W. Grignon
Master Taxidermist-Sculptor
RFD #1, U.S. Route 2
Pittsfield, ME 04967
Tel. (207) 487-2754

Forest Hart (Tobie)
Route 9
Hampden, ME 04444
Tel. (207) 862-4395

Moosehead Taxidermy
Harmony Village, ME 04942
Tel. (207) 683-2621

Northland Taxidermy
Box 195
Bennoch Road
Old Town, ME 04468
Tel. (207) 827-6168

Pond Town Taxidermy
  and Guides Choice
  Fly Shop
RFD #2, Box 7320
Winthrop, ME 04364
Tel. (207) 395-4358

Roberts' Taxidermy Studio
Ed Roberts
126 Thomaston Street
Rockland, ME 04841
Tel. (207) 594-4546

Spruce Hill Taxidermy
Heal Road
Lincolnville Center, ME 04850
Tel. (207) 763-4015

Dennis Therriault
Whicher's Mill Road
Sanford, ME 04073
Tel. (207) 324-8025

54 Indian Territory

As a result of the Maine Indian Land Claims Settlement Act of 1980, certain areas of the State have been designated Indian territory. The tribes owning these areas have exclusive authority to regulate hunting, trapping, and fishing. It may be necessary to obtain special permission or a license to hunt, trap, or fish in these areas.

PENOBSCOT NATION

In Franklin County—Alder Stream Twp.
In Penobscot County—T2R9 NWP (western portion), T3R9 NWP (eastern portion), T6R8 WELS (western portion), Argyle Twp. (northern portion) and T3R1 NBPP (northeastern portion). (Note: These areas will be conspicuously posted as Indian Territory).
In Piscataquis County—T6R8, NWP.

PASSAMAQUODDY TRIBE

In Franklin County—Lowelltown, T1R8, WBKP
In Hancock County—T4ND
In Washington County—T5ND, BPP; T19MD (Indian Twp.).
In Penobscot County—T5R1, NBPP
In Somerset County—Holeb T6R1 NBKP

Anyone wishing to hunt or trap on Indian territory should contact the appropriate Indian agency for further information:

```
Penobscot Indian Nation          Passamaquoddy Fish and
Dept. of Natural Resources          Game Dept.
Old Town, ME 04468               Box 301
Tel. (207) 827-7776,             Princeton, ME 04668
Ext. 230                         Tel. (207) 796-3501,
                                   Ext. 219

                 Passamaquoddy Fish
                   and Game Dept., WS
                 Pleasant Point, Box 343
                 Perry, ME 04667
                 Tel. (207) 853-2551,
                 Ext. 202
```

55 Sunrise and Sunset

Eastern Standard Time   Add one hour for Daylight Saving
Time, when in effect. It usually begins the last Sunday in
April and ends the last Sunday in October, each year.

Note   These are the times used by the Fish and Wildlife
Department to determine legal hunting and fishing hours.
They are valid for the remainder of the 20th Century.

	JAN.		FEB.		MAR.		APR.	
DAY	Rise A.M.	Set P.M.	Rise A.M.	Set P.M.	Rise A.M.	Set P.M.	Rise A.M.	Set P.M.
1	7 15	4 11	6 58	4 48	6 17	5 27	5 21	6 06
2	7 15	4 11	6 57	4 50	6 15	5 28	5 19	6 07
3	7 15	4 12	6 55	4 51	6 14	5 30	5 17	6 09
4	7 15	4 13	6 54	4 53	6 12	5 31	5 15	6 10
5	7 15	4 14	6 53	4 54	6 10	5 32	5 14	6 11
6	7 15	4 15	6 52	4 55	6 08	5 34	5 12	6 12
7	7 15	4 16	6 51	4 57	6 07	5 35	5 10	6 14
8	7 15	4 18	6 49	4 58	6 05	5 36	5 08	6 15
9	7 14	4 19	6 48	5 00	6 03	5 37	5 06	6 16
10	7 14	4 20	6 47	5 01	6 01	5 39	5 05	6 17
11	7 14	4 21	6 45	5 02	5 59	5 40	5 03	6 18
12	7 13	4 22	6 44	5 04	5 58	5 41	5 01	6 20
13	7 13	4 23	6 42	5 05	5 56	5 43	4 59	6 21
14	7 13	4 25	6 41	5 07	5 54	5 44	4 58	6 22
15	7 12	4 26	6 39	5 08	5 52	5 45	4 56	6 23
16	7 11	4 27	6 38	5 09	5 50	5 46	4 54	6 25
17	7 11	4 28	6 36	5 11	5 48	5 48	4 53	6 26
18	7 10	4 30	6 35	5 12	5 47	5 49	4 51	6 27
19	7 10	4 31	6 33	5 14	5 45	5 50	4 49	6 28
20	7 09	4 32	6 32	5 15	5 43	5 51	4 48	6 29
21	7 08	4 33	6 30	5 16	5 41	5 53	4 46	6 31
22	7 07	4 35	6 29	5 18	5 39	5 54	4 44	6 32
23	7 07	4 36	6 27	5 19	5 37	5 55	4 43	6 33
24	7 06	4 37	6 25	5 20	5 36	5 56	4 41	6 34
25	7 05	4 39	6 24	5 22	5 34	5 58	4 40	6 36
26	7 04	4 40	6 22	5 23	5 32	5 59	4 38	6 37
27	7 03	4 42	6 20	5 24	5 30	6 00	4 36	6 38
28	7 02	4 43	6 19	5 26	5 28	6 01	4 35	6 39
29	7 01	4 44	6 18	5 27	5 26	6 02	4 33	6 40
30	7 00	4 46			5 25	6 04	4 32	6 42
31	6 59	4 47			5 23	6 05		

DAY	MAY Rise A.M.	MAY Set P.M.	JUNE Rise A.M.	JUNE Set P.M.	JULY Rise A.M.	JULY Set P.M.	AUG. Rise A.M.	AUG. Set P.M.
1	4 30	6 43	3 58	7 16	3 59	7 27	4 26	7 04
2	4 29	6 44	3 58	7 17	3 59	7 27	4 27	7 03
3	4 28	6 45	3 57	7 18	4 00	7 27	4 28	7 02
4	4 26	6 46	3 57	7 18	4 00	7 26	4 29	7 00
5	4 25	6 48	3 56	7 19	4 01	7 26	4 30	6 59
6	4 23	6 49	3 56	7 20	4 02	7 26	4 32	6 58
7	4 22	6 50	3 56	7 21	4 02	7 25	4 33	6 56
8	4 21	6 51	3 55	7 21	4 03	7 25	4 34	6 55
9	4 20	6 52	3 55	7 22	4 04	7 24	4 35	6 54
10	4 18	6 54	3 55	7 22	4 05	7 24	4 36	6 52
11	4 17	6 55	3 55	7 23	4 05	7 23	4 37	6 51
12	4 16	6 56	3 55	7 24	4 06	7 23	4 38	6 49
13	4 15	6 57	3 54	7 24	4 07	7 22	4 40	6 48
14	4 14	6 58	3 54	7 24	4 08	7 22	4 41	6 46
15	4 12	6 59	3 54	7 25	4 09	7 21	4 42	6 45
16	4 11	7 00	3 54	7 25	4 10	7 20	4 43	6 43
17	4 10	7 01	3 54	7 26	4 11	7 19	4 44	6 41
18	4 09	7 03	3 54	7 26	4 11	7 19	4 45	6 40
19	4 08	7 04	3 55	7 26	4 12	7 18	4 46	6 38
20	4 07	7 05	3 55	7 27	4 13	7 17	4 48	6 37
21	4 06	7 06	3 55	7 27	4 14	7 16	4 49	6 35
22	4 05	7 07	3 55	7 27	4 15	7 15	4 50	6 33
23	4 05	7 08	3 55	7 27	4 16	7 14	4 51	6 32
24	4 04	7 09	3 56	7 27	4 17	7 13	4 52	6 30
25	4 03	7 10	3 56	7 27	4 18	7 12	4 53	6 28
26	4 02	7 11	3 56	7 27	4 19	7 11	4 55	6 27
27	4 01	7 12	3 57	7 27	4 21	7 10	4 56	6 25
28	4 01	7 13	3 57	7 27	4 22	7 09	4 57	6 23
29	4 00	7 13	3 58	7 27	4 23	7 08	4 58	6 21
30	3 59	7 14	3 58	7 27	4 24	7 07	4 59	6 20
31	3 59	7 15			4 25	7 05	5 00	6 18

DAY	SEPT.		OCT.		NOV.		DEC.	
	Rise A.M.	Set P.M.	Rise A.M.	Set P.M.	Rise A.M.	Set P.M.	Rise A.M.	Set P.M.
1	5 02	6 16	5 37	5 20	6 16	4 29	6 55	4 01
2	5 03	6 14	5 38	5 19	6 17	4 28	6 56	4 01
3	5 04	6 12	5 39	5 17	6 19	4 26	6 57	4 01
4	5 05	6 11	5 40	5 15	6 20	4 25	6 58	4 01
5	5 06	6 09	5 41	5 13	6 21	4 24	6 59	4 00
6	5 07	6 07	5 43	5 11	6 23	4 22	7 00	4 00
7	5 09	6 05	5 44	5 10	6 24	4 21	7 01	4 00
8	5 10	6 03	5 45	5 08	6 25	4 20	7 02	4 00
9	5 11	6 01	5 46	5 06	6 27	4 19	7 03	4 00
10	5 12	6 00	5 48	5 04	6 28	4 18	7 04	4 00
11	5 13	5 58	5 49	5 02	6 29	4 17	7 05	4 00
12	5 14	5 56	5 50	5 01	6 31	4 15	7 06	4 00
13	5 15	5 54	5 51	4 59	6 32	4 14	7 07	4 00
14	5 17	5 52	5 53	4 57	6 33	4 13	7 07	4 00
15	5 18	5 50	5 54	4 56	6 35	4 12	7 08	4 01
16	5 19	5 48	5 55	4 54	6 36	4 11	7 09	4 01
17	5 20	5 47	5 56	4 52	6 37	4 11	7 10	4 01
18	5 21	5 45	5 58	4 50	6 39	4 10	7 10	4 01
19	5 22	5 43	5 59	4 49	6 40	4 09	7 11	4 02
20	5 24	5 41	6 00	4 47	6 41	4 08	7 11	4 02
21	5 25	5 39	6 01	4 46	6 43	4 07	7 12	4 03
22	5 26	5 37	6 03	4 44	6 44	4 06	7 12	4 03
23	5 27	5 35	6 04	4 42	6 45	4 06	7 13	4 04
24	5 28	5 33	6 05	4 41	6 46	4 05	7 13	4 04
25	5 29	5 32	6 07	4 39	6 48	4 04	7 14	4 05
26	5 31	5 30	6 08	4 38	6 49	4 04	7 14	4 06
27	5 32	5 28	6 09	4 36	6 50	4 03	7 14	4 06
28	5 33	5 26	6 11	4 35	6 51	4 03	7 15	4 07
29	5 34	5 24	6 12	4 33	6 52	4 02	7 15	4 08
30	5 35	5 22	6 13	4 32	6 54	4 02	7 15	4 09
31			6 15	4 30			7 15	4 09

56 Hypothermia

Hypothermia is the greatest danger facing outdoors people in Maine. The usual causes of hypothermia are falling into the water while boating, or prolonged exposure to wind and cold while hunting. Life expectancy in 33–40 degree water is 15 minutes or less. A body loses heat 30 times faster in water than it does in the air.

The six steps of developing hypothermia take place as the body's inner core cools down. They are: 1. *shivering;* 2. *violent shivering, speech difficulty;* 3. *muscle stiffness, jerky movement, unclear thinking;* 4. *loss of contact with reality;* 5. *unconsciousness;* 6. *death.*

If you do fall out of a boat into the water, climb back into the boat and get as far out of the water as possible. Always wear a personal flotation device which will keep your head above water even if you become unconscious. If you must stay in the water, assume a fetal position and try to protect heat loss from the following areas: groin, armpits, neck, and head. Stay with the boat. It will make you easier to spot for rescuers. Remain as still as possible while awaiting rescue. You should only swim for shore if there is absolutely no chance of rescue and you are certain you can make it. Remember, in cold water you will lose coordination and become numb in under 10 minutes.

The key to preventing hypothermia while hunting is dressing properly, avoiding becoming wet or sweaty, eating plenty of high energy food, and staying well rested. Unlike falling in the water, it is wise to mix periods of exercise and rest when suffering from the first stages of hypothermia on land.

To prevent hypothermia wear proper clothing of wool,

high quality synthetic, or down for insulation. Tightly woven nylon or plastic provides wind protection. Cover your entire head first when cold and keep clothing dry of perspiration by ventilation. If your feet become cold, cover your head and hands as this aids circulation to the extremities.

Seek shelter before your strength subsides to the point of hindering movement. Trees, snow banks, bushes, or even a pile of leaves can provide shelter. Move slowly often; avoid running. If at all possible change into dry clothes.

Photo by Tom Carbone, courtesy of Maine Fish & Game Department.

QUICK REFERENCE INDEX